21世纪经济与管理应用型本科规划教材
国际经济与贸易系列

外贸函电

Business Correspondence
in International

宋亚坤 杨春梅 编著

图书在版编目(CIP)数据

外贸函电/宋亚坤,杨春梅编著. —北京:北京大学出版社,2012.2
(21世纪经济与管理应用型本科规划教材·国际经济与贸易系列)
ISBN 978-7-301-20175-6

Ⅰ.①外… Ⅱ.①宋… ②杨… Ⅲ.①对外贸易—英语—电报信函—高等学校—教材 Ⅳ.①H315

中国版本图书馆CIP数据核字(2012)第018046号

书　　　　名:	外贸函电
著作责任者:	宋亚坤　杨春梅　编著
策 划 编 辑:	马　霄
责 任 编 辑:	马　霄
标 准 书 号:	ISBN 978-7-301-20175-6/F·3043
出 　版 　者:	北京大学出版社
地　　　　址:	北京市海淀区成府路205号　100871
网　　　　址:	http://www.pup.cn
电　　　　话:	邮购部 62752015　发行部 62750672　编辑部 62752926　出版部 62754962
电 子 信 箱:	em@pup.cn
印 　刷 　者:	三河市博文印刷有限公司
发 　行 　者:	北京大学出版社
经 　销 　者:	新华书店
	730毫米×1020毫米　16开本　12印张　227千字
	2012年3月第1版　2014年7月第2次印刷
印　　　　数:	4001—6000册
定　　　　价:	25.00元

未经许可,不得以任何方式复制或抄袭本书之部分或全部内容。

版权所有,侵权必究

举报电话:010-62752024；电子信箱:fd@pup.pku.edu.cn

丛书出版前言

《国家中长期教育改革和发展规划纲要(2010—2020年)》指出,目前我国高等教育还不能完全适应国家经济社会发展的要求,学生适应社会和就业创业能力不强,创新型、实用型、复合型人才紧缺。所以,在此背景下,北京大学出版社响应教育部号召,在整合和优化课程、推进课程精品化与网络化的基础上,积极构建与实践接轨、与研究生教育接轨、与国际接轨的本科教材体系,特策划出版《21世纪经济与管理应用型本科规划教材》。

《21世纪经济与管理应用型本科规划教材》注重系统性与综合性,注重加强学生分析能力、人文素养及应用性技能的培养。本系列包含三类课程教材:通识课程教材,如《大学生创业指导》等,着重于提高学生的全面素质;基础课程教材,如《经济学原理》《管理学基础》等,着重于培养学生建立宽厚的学科知识基础;专业课程教材,如《组织行为学》《市场营销学》等,着重于培养学生扎实的学科专业知识以及动手能力和创新意识。

本系列教材在编写中注重增加相关内容以支持教师在课堂中使用先进的教学手段和多元化的教学方法,如用课堂讨论资料帮助教师进行启发式教学,增加案例及相关资料引发学生的学习兴趣等;并坚持用精品课程建设的标准来要求各门课程教材的编写,力求配套多元的教辅资料,如电子课件、习题答案和案例分析要点等。

为使本系列教材具有持续的生命力,我们每隔三年左右会对教材进行一次修订。我们欢迎所有使用本系列教材的师生给我们提出宝贵的意见和建议(我们的电子邮箱是 em@pup.cn),您的关注就是我们不断进取的动力。

在此,感谢所有参与编写和为我们出谋划策提供帮助的专家学者,以及广大使用本系列教材的师生,希望本系列教材能够为我国高等院校经管专业的教育贡献绵薄之力。

北京大学出版社
经济与管理图书事业部
2012年1月

前　　言

  本教材主要针对大学本科及以上国际经济与贸易相关专业的学生，在教材定位、编排体例、主导思想和具体内容安排上有所创新，同时吸收了以往外贸函电教材的精华，实现兼容并蓄。

  本教材突破了传统的单纯外贸专业英语教材的定位，将外贸函电课程的学习过程看成对先导国际贸易专业课的梳理、归纳和仿真实践过程，提供完整鲜明的业务主线，概括相关信件的法律意义。

  编排内容时，本书以业务过程和法律权利义务为两条线索，将松散的业务信函串联起来，兼顾业务的整体连贯性和现实情况的多样性，既有仿真演示，又有充实的例信库。兼顾英文业务术语、信函写作的学习与其背后的法律内涵，既详解重点用语的用法，又阐述这些信函所涉及的法律权利与义务关系。

  通过对本教材的学习，学生的写作能力、专业英语能力、业务知识和相关的法律知识运用能力都可以得到锻炼和提高。

  全书分三大模块：

1. 写作方法

  介绍外贸业务信函的写作目的、原则、格式以及如何开头结尾，配以具体形象的实例。

2. 仿真流程

  绘制国际货物贸易中以信用证方式结算的CIF合同从洽谈到履行的完整流程图；并以一笔交易为例，附上各环节的单据、信函，配以简要的流程说明。

3. 主要外贸业务环节业务信函详解

  分为建立业务关系、合同的达成、合同的履行与争议的解决四大部分。引用相关公约、惯例或法规，简要说明各环节的法律权利义务；附上代表性的例信，介绍信函体例、专业术语；章后练习以翻译和情境写作为主，既兼顾基础知识又注重考查学生的应用能力。

  本教材在编写过程中，承蒙外贸企业朋友提供案例及单证，并吸取以往外贸函电相关教材的精华，在此表示诚挚的谢意。由于经验及水平所限，教材仍存在不足之处，欢迎指正。

编　者
2012年1月

目 录 Contents

◆ 第一单元　写作方法 / 1

　　　　　第一章　外贸业务信函的写作方法 / 3

◆ 第二单元　仿真流程 / 13

　　　　　第二章　外贸业务流程及相关信函、单证演示 / 15

◆ 第三单元　建立业务关系 / 81

　　　　　第三章　建立业务关系与资信调查 / 83

◆ 第四单元　合同的达成 / 91

　　　　　第四章　要约邀请 / 93
　　　　　第五章　要约 / 99
　　　　　第六章　承诺、反要约与拒绝 / 108
　　　　　第七章　合同书 / 120

◆ 第五单元　合同的履行 / 129

　　　　　第八章　运输与保险 / 131
　　　　　第九章　支付 / 144

◆ 第六单元　争议的解决 / 157

　　　　　第十章　索赔理赔 / 159

◆ 课后练习题部分参考答案 / 172

◆ 参考文献 / 184

第一单元 写作方法

第一章　外贸业务信函的写作方法

一、外贸业务信函及其写作目的

外贸业务信函，是在国际货物贸易中联系客户、与交易伙伴洽谈合同，或就合同履行的程序与问题交换信息的往来书信。外贸业务信函既可以是传统的纸质信函、传真，也可以是现代的网络电子文书。

外贸业务信函属于商业书信的范畴。它不同于私人信件，更不同于小说、散文，不追求华丽的辞藻，更不需要渲染气氛和感情。得体、准确、充分、简洁地沟通信息是外贸业务信函追求的首要目标。只有这样才能保障交易的顺利进行，使交易各方共同受益。

二、外贸业务信函的写作原则

敏锐的商业眼光可以帮助企业发现商机；而商场上的人情练达、厚德载物才能保证企业的持续和长远发展。商务信函字里行间透露着写信人的业务素养和人格特质。书写外贸业务信函，应秉承互利共赢的原则，遵循国际交易规则，及时、充分、简洁地与对方沟通一切必要的业务信息，以确保交易顺畅、平稳、高效地进行。

这里提出外贸业务信函写作的"6C"原则，以供参考。

1. 体谅（consideration）

市场经济以交换为特征，通过满足他人的需求以实现自身的价值。互利共赢、适者生存是市场经济生态圈的生存法则。换位思考、把握市场需求、在自身盈利与市场需求之间谋求平衡，是这一生态圈中每个成员的必修课。

体谅是外贸信函写作必须把握的第一原则，体谅意味着尊重合作伙伴、换位思考、讲求双方利益平衡。在具体的写作过程中，要体现真诚合作的态度；要尽可能从收信人的立场来考虑问题，在分析对方会如何理解信息的基础上，提供其所需要的信息；要坚持用肯定而非否定的态度。

试比较下面几组例句：

---

① a. I write to send my congratulations.
　　b. Congratulations to you on your promotion!
② a. Your letter is not clear at all. I can't understand it.
　　b. If I understand your letter correctly....
③ a. We won't be able to send you the brochure this month.
　　b. We will send you the brochure next month.

---

④ a. We regret that you closed your account with us a week ago.
b. A week ago you closed your account with us. Whatever the reason, we are pleased to have played some small part in your program. You are cordially invited to use our other services if occasion may require.

即使是索赔函,买方因卖方发错货而遭到不必要的麻烦,也应该体现出合作和体谅的精神。见下面的例子:

Dear Sirs,
　　We have received your goods covering our order No. 555 of May 5th. Upon opening the cases we found case No. 99 contained completely different articles.
　　As we are in urgent need of the articles, we ask you to arrange for the dispatch of the replacements at once.
　　A list of the contents of the wrongly dispatched case is attached. Please let us know what you want us to do with them.
Sincerely yours

2. 遵循国际规则(conformity to international practice)

外贸业务以及与之相关的国际货物运输、保险、国际支付等,因其涉外性质,必须遵守国际规则;而这些领域的国际公约和惯例也较集中。

自19世纪以来,国际经济、文化及其他民事交往迅速发展,为了满足国际贸易的迅速发展对于稳定性、可预见性的期望,主权国家纷纷签订或缔结含有大量实体规范的双边或多边条约,直接具体地确定国际贸易相关当事人的权利义务。主要有:①关于国际货物买卖的《联合国国际货物销售合同公约》(1980年),我国于1986年核准。②调整提单运输的《海牙规则》(1924年)、《维斯比规则》(1968年)和《汉堡规则》(1978年),以及2008年12月11日,联合国大会正式通过的《联合国全程或部分海上国际货物运输合同公约》,即《鹿特丹规则》。③调整国际货物航空运输的《华沙公约》(1929年)、《海牙议定书》(1955年),我国分别于1958年和1975年加入;《蒙特利尔公约》(1999年),2005年7月31日正式对我国生效。④国际铁路货物运输主要适用的两个公约《国际铁路货物联运协定》(1951年)(简称《国际货协》)和《关于铁路货物运输的国际公约》(1938年)(简称《国际货约》),我国是《国际货协》的成员国。

同时,在国际贸易中,经过反复实践形成许多习惯做法,一些国际民间组织将其编纂成国际惯例,在国际贸易实践中具有广泛的指导作用。国际惯例一旦得到国家的承认并由当事人选用,就对当事人具有法律约束力。主要有:①国际商会就常见的贸易术语制定的统一解释规则《国际贸易术语解释通则》,该惯例历经多次修改,最新的版本是2010年修改本,即Incoterms® 2010,于2011年1月1日起生效实施;与此同时,当事人仍可选择使用Incoterms® 2000。②国际商会于1958年草拟通过、1979年1月1日生效的《托收统一规则》。③国际商会于1930年拟定、1933年正式公布,经过6次修改的《跟单信用证统一惯例》,最后将2007年的修改以"600号"出版物公布。

各国国内立法一般都规定国际条约优先适用以及国际惯例的补缺原则。例如,我国《民法通则》第142条第2款规定:"中华人民共和国缔结或参加的国际条约同中华人民共和国民事法律有不同规定的,适用国际条约的规定,但中华人民共和国声明保留的条款除外。"该条第3款规定:"中华人民共和国法律或中华人民共和国缔结或参加的国际条约没有规定的,可以适用国际惯例。"

国际惯例虽然理论上不具备强制约束力,但由于得到相关参与方的广泛引用,成为事实上的法律。

在国际货物贸易中,从事相关工作的人员要熟悉这些国际规则的内容,依据国际通行做法运作日常业务。书写外贸业务信函,相关的内容必须使用统一规范的术语和表达方式,以提高沟通效率,避免歧义。

例如,使用跟单信用证进行结算时,买卖双方应明确的内容主要有:开证申请人、开证银行、开证时间、信用证种类、信用证金额、信用证到期地点和到期日等。下面是通常的表达方式:

> The buyer shall open through a bank acceptable to the seller an irrevocable letter of credit payable at 45 days' sight for 100% of the contract value to reach the seller 30 days before the month of shipment and valid for negotiation in China until the 15th day after the date of shipment.

再如,以CIF、CIP作为贸易术语的合同中,保险条款是合同的主要条款之一。保险条款包含的要素主要有:何方办理保险、保险金额、保险险别、按什么保险条款保险。可以借鉴下面的例句:

> Insurance: To be covered by the Seller for 110% of total invoice value against All Risks and War Risks as per and subject to the relevant ocean marine cargo clauses of the People's Insurance Company of China dated 1/1/1981.

在国际贸易中,每个业务环节都有相应的术语和相对固定的表达方式,熟练地掌握这些术语和表达方式,有助于我们事半功倍地掌握英文外贸信函的写法。更重要的是,在日常业务沟通中使用统一规范的表达方式,可以减少误解,提高沟通效率。

3. 清楚(clarity)

外贸业务信函,应主题鲜明、层次清晰,没有晦涩难懂或易产生误会之处,使读者一目了然。

　　写作前，写信人要明确写作主题，列出写作纲要，谋篇布局，合理划分段落，必要时使用主题行点明全篇写作主题。

　　遣词造句，尽量选用简短、熟悉和口语化的词语；将句中彼此联系紧密的成分放在一起。

　　比较下面几组词语和句子：

词语

after	subsequent
issue	promulgate
house	domicile
daily	per diem
well acquainted	au fait
the present position	status quo
We can deliver…	We are in a position to deliver…
If you decide to…	If you come to a decision to…
according to	as per

句子

Those who work rapidly get ill in those conditions.

Those who work in these conditions rapidly get ill.

The L/C must reach us for arranging shipment not later than 8 October.

The L/C must reach us not later than 8 October for arranging shipment.

---

4. 具体（concreteness）

　　具体形象的文字才有说服力，才能引起读者的共鸣。"危楼高千尺，手可摘星辰。不敢高声语，恐惊天上人。"诗仙李白正是用了夸张的手法，才引起人们无数绮丽的想象；马致远的乡愁也因为着落在"枯藤老树昏鸦，小桥流水人家，古道西风瘦马"身上，才跨越时空，历经近千年仍在现代人的心头回响。

　　对于外贸业务信函，"具体"意味着以事实和数据说话。介绍产品和公司时，切忌主观臆断、盲目下结论，必须以事实和数据作支撑；安排业务进程时，要具体、可操作。否则，或者给人留下夸夸其谈、不负责任的印象，或者延误了业务的进程，造成不必要的损失。

　　比较下面两组句子：

---

① a. By integrating this revolutionary new machine into your manufacturing system, we feel sure your production volume can be substantially increased.

> b. Without any increase in electric power consumption it gives out 15% more heat than earlier models, you will find in the price list particulars of our terms printed on the inside front cover of the catalogue.
>
> ② a. Our brake is very efficient.
> b. Our Jason Brand brake can stop a two – ton car within 2 feet.

5. 简洁(conciseness)

商务信函,力求言简意赅。有人将"清明时节雨纷纷,路上行人欲断魂。"简化为:"清明雨纷纷,行人欲断魂"。抛开韵律美,后一句话确实用更短的语言传达了同样的信息。商务信函,在不遗漏具体信息,无损于书信的完整和礼貌的前提下,要尽量使用最简短的语言。

比较下面几组句子:

> ① a. We have begun to <u>export</u> our machines to <u>countries abroad</u>.
> b. We have begun to <u>export</u> our machines.
> ② a. <u>In the event that</u> you speak to Mr. Wood <u>in regard to</u> production, ask him to <u>give consideration to</u> the delivery schedule.
> b. <u>If</u> you speak to Mr. Wood <u>about</u> production, ask him to <u>consider</u> the delivery schedule.
> ③ a. We require furniture <u>which is of the new type</u>.
> b. We require <u>new – type</u> furniture.
> ④ a. <u>It should be noted that</u> this is the best we can do. (本句划线的部分删去)
> b. <u>Please be advised that</u> we have received your invoice. (本句划线的部分删去)

简洁不等于短,下面一组句子中,虽然第一句更短,但遗漏了必要的信息:

> a. We enclose a copy of maintenance manual you asked for in your letter.
> b. We enclose a copy of <u>our E – 30 Air Condition</u> maintenance manual which you asked for in your letter <u>of May 5th</u>.

去掉不必要的词语和冗长的句子,保留有效、简洁的事实信息,就可以把最重要的信息呈现给对方。

6. 完整(completeness)

一封业务信函必须包含所有必要的信息,发出之前要认真检查。

三、外贸业务信函的格式

1. 外贸业务信函的格式

外贸业务信函主要有两种格式:齐头式和缩行式。

(1) 齐头式

所有内容,包括地址、日期、称呼、正文、结尾致意等均左起书写;正文段落开始不空格,以段间空行作为划分段落的标志。见下例:

```
OMNICORP INTERNATIONAL
17 Bunder Hill Road                          ----------------(1)
Shrewsbury MA01545
Tel 03 – 3456788 Fax 34567


June 3, 2009                                 ----------------(2)


Mr. R. Jameson
25 Silverthon Gardens
BATH Somerset                                ----------------(3)
BA2 9AN
Britain


Dear Mr. Jameson,                            ----------------(4)


Filing system catalogues                     ----------------(5)


We are grateful for these copies of your current catalogues. We are particularly inter-
ested in filing cabinets.                    ----------------(6)


Yours sincerely,                             ----------------(7)


BD Davis                                     ----------------(8)
Managing Director
```

(2) 缩行式

内容安排错落有致,段落起始空四格。如下例:

> February 15, 2009
>
> Dr. David Peters
> State Insurance Corporation
> 345 Hightower Boulevard
> Prince Town, US 12345
>
> Dear Dr. Peters,
>
> SUBJECT: Applying for a position
>
> I should like to apply for the position of advertising manager which you advertised this morning. I am 27 years old and I graduated from Leeds University with an honours degree in English.
>
> I should very much like to take the opportunity to work in industry and I hope you will feel able to give me an interview.
>
> Very truly yours,
J. P. Harvey

2. 外贸业务信函的组成部分

外贸业务信函通常由六部分组成：信头、信内地址、称呼、正文、结尾套语、签署及其他选择性项目，包括主题、附件等。

现以齐头式例信为例，逐一说明：

(1) 信头

主要内容是发信人公司名称、地址、联系方式等。地址按从小到大的顺序分别写明公司名称、门牌号和街道、城市和邮编、所在国家。

印就格式的信头通常在信纸上部正中央，也可位于右上角或左上角。如使用空白信纸，信头应打印于信纸右上角或左上角。

(2) 日期

日期位于信头下方，空行书写。

日期的写法主要有两种，如：8 June, 2009 或 June 8, 2009。最好不要用简写的形式，如：Dec. 8, 2009。此外，各国日期的写法习惯不同，美式的写法为月/日/年，英式写法为日/月/年。因此应避免使用纯数字表示日期，如：2/3/2009，以防产生误解和歧义。

(3) 信内地址

收信人的公司名称和地址。日期之后空行书写，按顺序依次打印收信人的公司名称、门牌号、街道名称、城市名、邮编及国家。

(4) 称呼

称呼用语取决于发信人和收信人的关系。商务信函中，常用的正式称呼用语有

"Dear Sir（Madam）",或"Dear Sirs（Mesdames）",或美国人较常用的"Gentlemen"。目前,人们倾向于采用非正式的称呼用语。当收信人与发信人彼此相识时,应使用类似"Dear Mr. Jameson"这样更为亲切的称呼。

（5）主题

在信件较长,或涉及内容较多时,用主题行提示信函的主要内容可以帮助收信人快速把握信件主题,提高阅读效率。标题第一个字母或主要词的第一个字母要大写。

（6）正文

正文是信的主体,商业信函讲究清晰明了,因此段落宜短不宜长。

（7）结尾致意

常见的结尾致意用语有 Sincerely,Yours sincerely,Sincerely yours,Yours truly,Truly yours,Very truly yours,Yours faithfully,Faithfully yours。一般来说,只有在不清楚收信人姓名的情况下,才用 Yours faithfully,Faithfully yours 作结尾致意。

（8）签名

签名表示当事人的意思表示,且与写信人的身份唯一对应,具有法律效力的文件必须经意思表示人签署,外贸业务信函信末必须用水笔手写签名。

由于手写体签名不易辨认,通常在手写体下打印签名者姓名,同时要注明发信人所代表的公司和任职职位。例如:

Yours faithfully,

For The Overseas Co., Ltd

（sgd）

W. Black

President

四、外贸业务信函的开头与结尾

1. 外贸业务信函的开头

好的开头是成功的一半。外贸业务信函一般都这样开始:

（1）说明写信的动机与目的。例如:

---

① We understand that you are exporters of nuts & kernels and should like to know if you can supply us with 5 tons walnut meat by the end of October.

② We read with interest your advertisement in the China Daily and should be glad to receive particulars of your tender for port construction.

（2）讨论收信人最关切的问题。例如：
I'm pleased to tell you that your order will be delivered tomorrow.
比较下面一组句子：

> a. This is to tell you about our shipping problems.
> b. We are pleased to tell you that your order 167 was dispatched yesterday.

（3）提及上封信的日期和大致内容。比较下面一组句子：

> a. This is in reply to your letter of June 5.
> b. Thank you for your interest in our electric heaters, expressed in your letter of June 5.

2. 外贸业务信函的结尾

结尾通常用来总结信的内容或者安排下一步的行动。

（1）结尾要具体，避免言之无物或陈词滥调。如：

① <u>Hoping to hear</u> from you <u>at your earliest convenience</u>.

② <u>Do not hesitate to</u> contact us if you have any question.

相反，可以强调信中提到的具体事项，如：

We hope to hear soon about our shipment.

比较下面一组句子：

> a. We should be pleased if you would respond to our request at your earliest convenience.
> b. Please send us your illustrated catalogue and price list soon.

（2）做下一步安排，如：

① We hope we may have your decision soon.

② Please send us these forms by October 2nd.

比较下面一组句子：

> a. We are sure these forms will enable you to obtain admission to the school.
> b. Please send in the forms not later than February 5th.

（3）利用结尾作总结，特别是对于长的、复杂的信而言。
试比较下面两种结尾哪个更有效：

a. We hope that we have made the above alternatives clear to you and that they may help you to make your choice.
b. To sum up, you can either put your money in a savings bank and receive 6% annual interest, or invest in common stocks for higher returns but also higher risk.

第二单元 仿真流程

第二章　外贸业务流程及相关信函、单证演示

　　以信用证方式结算的国际货物买卖，程序相对复杂。本章绘制了以信用证结算的国际货物买卖 CIF 合同的洽谈和履行流程图，并以一宗实际业务为例，依次附上各环节的主要单据和信函，为全书的内容勾勒一个完整、具体的框架。

　　对外贸业务的全过程了然于胸，才能统筹安排，防患于未然，最大限度地保证交易的平稳运行、一气呵成，避免措手不及、节外生枝，造成不必要的人力、物力、财力和时间的浪费。

　　书写每个环节的业务信函，都要有整体意识和过程意识。本章的安排正是希望描绘一条线索，勾勒一个框架。在交易过程中，由于商品性质、交易对手、交易方式等不同，交易细节会千差万别，本章所构造的框架正是提取了各种情况下交易的共性，试图概括性地描述外贸业务交易过程。

　　具体来看，在进行业务洽谈时，要综合考虑商品性质、交易对手、国际交易习惯和有关国家的宏观监管政策等，统筹安排所有交易条款，达成互利和可操作的合同，降低交易风险。

　　合同执行的过程中，交易双方也要从整体把握，控制好每个环节的业务风险，以 CIF 信用证合同为例：

　　出口商审核信用证要以合同为主要依据；在托运、报检、投保、报关、出运等环节，虽然主要与国内的贸易服务企业、贸易管理部门打交道，也要时刻牢记信用证与合同的要求，使反馈单据与信用证要求一致，确保顺利结汇；在买方付款之前，确保对物权、保险索赔权等的控制。

　　进口方申请开立信用证要以合同为依据，避免不必要的修改；同时，关键的业务环节，如对货物品质、数量的检验，交货装运等，要重视相应的单据要求，确保在单据买卖的情况下控制卖方的实际履约行为。

　　此外，在整个交易过程中，双方还要就交易进程及时沟通信息，做好单证、货物的交接。图 2.1 是以信用证结算的国际货物买卖 CIF 合同的洽谈和履行程序示意图。

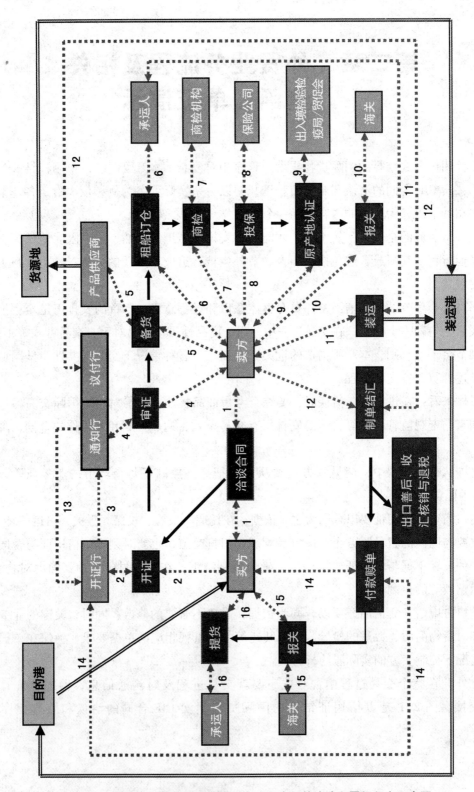

图2.1 以信用证结算的国际货物买卖CIF合同的洽谈和履行程序示意图

图注：■表示以信用证结算的国际货物买卖的业务环节。即买卖双方为了完成一笔国际货物买卖，需要处理的事务和办理的手续。

▨表示国际货物买卖涉及的相关当事人，包括买卖双方，产品供应商（有时只有卖方）；提供结算、融资、运输、保险、商检等服务的银行、承运人、保险公司、商检机构等其他企业；海关等贸易管理机关。

→表示事务流。即事务的先后顺序，通常情况，从双方洽谈合同开始，到买方最终提货结束。示意图中同时以序号标出顺序。

⇢表示信息流。买卖双方为完成交易，相互之间，以及与其他有关各方交换信息，包括单证传递。

⇒表示物流。货物的流向，从货源地，经由装运港，运往目的港、目的地。

这部分以天津天宝服装进出口有限公司（以下简称天宝公司）与日本客户的男式睡衣买卖为例，结合图 2.1 所示的交易流程，说明各业务环节信函和涉及的主要相关单据。

1. 洽谈合同

交易双方通过要约、承诺，就商品、品质、数量、价格、交货地点、日期和方式、支付方式、保险等达成一致的意思表示，合同成立。

洽谈过程中，要明确自身信函的目的，并判断对方的订约意图。区分要约与要约邀请，接受、还盘与拒绝。不同性质的函件对双方的订约约束力不同。

合同是双方的执行依据。在洽谈时，要综合考虑商品性质、交易对手、国际交易习惯和有关国家的宏观监管政策等，统筹安排所有交易条款，达成互利和可操作的合同，降低交易风险。

（1）2011 年 4 月 15 日，天宝公司业务员从《国际商报》上看到一则消息"日本一公司求购中国全棉睡衣"，遂与该报回音台取得联系，得知该公司具体联系方式，发出建立业务关系函。（第 18 页）

（2）2011 年 4 月 19 日，天宝公司收到了 Kaneyoshi 公司的询盘函，即要约邀请。（第 19 页）

（3）4 月 21 日天宝公司发出发盘函，此函十分确定并且表明发盘人在得到接受时承受约束的意旨，规定有效期，根据《联合国国际货物销售合同公约》的精神是一项不可撤销的要约。（第 20 页）

（4）4 月 23 日，天宝公司收到 Kaneyoshi 公司的还盘函，还盘函对价格和支付条件提出修改，可视为一项新要约。（第 21 页）

（5）4 月 24 日，天宝公司还盘，提出新的价格和并强调对新的客户必须使用信用证支付条件。（第 22 页）

（6）2011 年 4 月 26 日，天宝公司收到 Kaneyoshi 公司的来函和订单，进一步明确在 6 月底前交货。（第 23、24 页）

（7）天宝公司审核订单后，发现货号 538A 的订购数量与货物包装方式不符。为遵循客户等量拼装的原则，天宝公司决定将其数量调整至 4950 件，并接受客户的其他交易条件，向 Kaneyoshi 公司寄送售货确认书。（第 25、26、27 页）

天津天宝服装进出口有限公司
Tianjin Tianbao Garment I/E Co., Ltd

15th-Apr-2011

Mr. Genichiro Sata
Kaneyoshi Co., Ltd.
14-22 Kyomachi-Bori 2-Chome
Nishi-Ku, Kobe, JAPAN
Tel:06-6441-3325 Fax:06-6445-2391

Dear Mr. Sata,

From the April 15th issue of the International Business Daily we have learned that you are in the market for 100% cotton Pajamas, which just fall within our business scope. We are now writing to you with a hope to establish long-term trade relations.

We have been in the line of garment export for more than 20 years and have good connections with some reputable garment factories. Therefore sufficient supplies and on-time delivery are guaranteed.

Enclosed please find our latest catalogue for pajamas, which may meet with your demand. You'll see they are all made of high quality materials with exquisite workmanship. Actually they have been well accepted by many Japanese buyers.

In addition, we can also produce according to your designated styles so long as the quantity is substantial. If you have any specific requirements, please just let us know.

As to our financial standing, you may refer to the Bank of China, Tianjin Branch (26 Nanjing Road, Hexi District, Tianjin, China Tel:+88-22-23177089).We will appreciate it if you could inform us of your bank reference.

We are pleased to add you to our list of clients and look forward to your enquiries.

Yours sincerely,
Tianjin Tianbao Garment I/E Co.,Ltd

Deng Xin

Encl. Catalogue

中国天津和平区岳阳道 66 号
No.66 Yueyang Road, Heping District, Tianjin 300140, China
电话/Tel:86-22-58818844   传真/Fax:86-22-58818766   网址/Web: www.Tianbao.com.cn

Kaneyoshi Co., Ltd.
14-22 Kyomachi-Bori 2-Chome
Nishi-Ku, Kobe, JAPAN
Tel:06-6441-3325
Fax:06-6445-2391

Apr. 19th, 2011

Mr. Deng Xin
Tianjin Tianbao Garment I/E Co., Ltd.
No.66 Yueyang Road, Heping District,
Tianjin 300140, China

Dear Mr.Deng,

We are pleased to receive your mail of April 15th and your catalogue.

We are large dealers in leisurewear. Demand for 100% cotton garment is increasing recently in Japan and there is a promising market here for moderately priced garments.

After studying your catalogue, we are particularly interested in the following items: Men's Pajama Trousers Article No.538A and Men's Night Shirt Article No.538B.

Please quote us your best CIF Kobe prices for the above-mentioned items both on 20'FCL and LCL basis as well as your terms of shipment, payment and insurance.

Meanwhile we would like to have some samples to test the market demand before we could place a firm order.

If the market reactions are good, and your prices are competitive, we'd certainly be able to place a substantial order.

For your information, our banker is The Minato Bank Ltd., (2-1-1, Sannomiya-cho, Chuo-ku, Kobe, 651-0193 Japan Tel:+ 06-6455-3465). We hope to hear from you soon.

Yours truly,
Kaneyoshi Co., Ltd.

Genichiro Sata
Genichiro Sata

天津天宝服装进出口有限公司
Tianjin Tianbao Garment I/E Co., Ltd

21st -Apr-2011

Mr. Genichiro Sata
Kaneyoshi Co., Ltd.
14-22 Kyomachi-Bori 2-Chome
Nishi-Ku, Kobe, JAPAN

Dear Mr. Sata,

We are pleased to have received your enquiry of April 19th and the samples you asked for will be sent to you by separate post.

We think you have made an excellent choice in selecting the two items, and once you have seen the samples we are sure you will be impressed by the quality of materials and workmanship.

As requested, we would like to quote our favorable prices as follows:

Art No.	Commodity	Min.Order Quantity	Unit Price CIF Kobe	
			20'FCL Basis	LCL Basis
538A	Men's Pajama Trousers (100% cotton)	1000 pieces	USD4.6/piece	USD5.0/piece
538B	Men's Night Shirt (100% cotton)	1000 pieces	USD5.3/piece	USD6.0/piece

Packing: 538A: 100pcs/ctn, 150ctns/20'FCL
538B: 50pcs/ctn, 150ctns/20'FCL

Payment: By sight L/C.

Shipment: To be effected within 30 days from receipt of the relevant L/C.

Insurance: For 110% invoice value covering All Risks and War Risks.

Because of fluctuating exchange rates, we can only hold these prices for three weeks from today's date.

We believe you will find a ready sale for our products in Japan as have other retailers in your country and we hope we can reach an agreement on the terms quoted.

Thank you for your interest; we look forward to hearing from you soon.

Yours sincerely,
Tianjin Tianbao Garment I/E Co., Ltd

Deng Xin

中国天津和平区岳阳道 66 号
No.66 Yueyang Road, Heping District, Tianjin 300140, China
电话/Tel:86-22-58818844   传真/Fax:86-22-58818766   网址/Web: www.Tianbao.com.cn

Kaneyoshi Co., Ltd.
14-22 Kyomachi-Bori 2-Chome
Nishi-Ku, Kobe, JAPAN
Tel:06-6441-3325
Fax:06-6445-2391

April 23rd, 2011

Mr. Deng Xin
Tianjin Tianbao Garment I/E Co., Ltd.
No.66 Yueyang Road, Heping District,
Tianjin 300140, China

Dear Mr.Deng,

We are glad to receive your offer of April 21st and relative samples.

In reply, we regret to say that your prices are not competitive enough. Information here indicates that 100% Cotton Pajamas from other suppliers sold about 5% lower than yours.

We really appreciate the good workmanship and materials of your products, but are also aware that the price level counts much, especially in the initial sales stage.

To set up the trade, may we suggest you give a special discount as follows:

538A USD4.3/piece
538B USD5.0/piece
CIF Kobe on 20'FCL basis

Meanwhile, we usually deal with our clients on D/P terms, which is easier and cost-saving than L/C. We hope that method of payment will be acceptable to you also.

Actually, competitive prices and flexible payment terms for a trial order can often lead to a big market share with great profit in the future. We hope you will take this factor into account and wait for your early reply.

Yours truly,
Kaneyoshi Co., Ltd.
Genichiro Sata
Genichiro Sata

天津天宝服装进出口有限公司
Tianjin Tianbao Garment I/E Co., Ltd

24th-April-2011

Mr. Genichiro Sata
Kaneyoshi Co., Ltd.
14-22 Kyomachi-Bori 2-Chome
Nishi-Ku, Kobe, JAPAN

Dear Mr. Sata,

We are pleased to receive your mail of April 23rd.

Much to our regret, we find it impossible to comply with your request. Your offer is too low and cannot serve as a basis for further negotiation with our manufacturers. As you might be aware, materials prices and wages have risen considerably these days. The prices we quoted on April 21st were very favorable if you take the quality and workmanship into consideration. It is really hard for us to make further concession.

However, in order to develop our market in your area, we have decided to give you an exceptional offer as follows:

CIF Kobe on 20'FCL basis
Article No.538A   USD4.5/piece
Article No.538B   USD5.2/piece

Other conditions remained unchanged.

We have noted your request for D/P terms. Unfortunately our company never offer documentary collection terms to customers until they have traded with us for over a year. We are really sorry that we cannot be more helpful at present.

In view of the heavy demand for this line, we advise you to place an order at your earliest convenience if prompt shipment is required.

We look forward to your favorable reply.

Yours sincerely,
Tianjin Tianbao Garment I/E Co., Ltd

Deng Xin

中国天津和平区岳阳道 66 号
No.66 Yueyang Road, Heping District, Tianjin 300140, China
电话/Tel:86-22-58818844   传真/Fax:86-22-58818766   网址/Web: www.Tianbao.com.cn

Kaneyoshi Co., Ltd.
14-22 Kyomachi-Bori 2-Chome
Nishi-Ku, Kobe, JAPAN
Tel:06-6441-3325
Fax:06-6445-2391

April 26th, 2011

Mr. Deng Xin
Tianjin Tianbao Garment I/E Co., Ltd.
No.66 Yueyang Road, Heping District,
Tianjin 300140, China

Dear Mr.Deng,

Your letter of April 24th convinced us to place at least a trial order for your pajamas. We enclose our order No.KANT-11-0426.

We have decided to accept your prices and terms of payment by sight L/C, but would like these terms to be reviewed in the near future.

We would appreciate delivery within June, and look forward to receiving your Sales Confirmation.

Yours truly,
Kaneyoshi Co., Ltd.
Genichiro Sata
Genichiro Sata

Kaneyoshi Co., Ltd.
14-22 Kyomachi-Bori 2-Chome
Nishi-Ku, Kobe, JAPAN
Tel:06-6441-3325
Fax:06-6445-2391

PURCHASE ORDER

No.: KANT-11-0426
Date: April 26th, 2011

To: Tianjin Tianbao Garment I/E Co., Ltd.
No.66 Yueyang Road, Heping District,
Tianjin 300140, China

Item Description	Quantity	Price
		CIF Kobe
538A Men's Pajama Trousers (100% cotton)	21900 pieces	USD4.50/piece
538B Men's Night Shirts (100% cotton)	4960 pieces	USD5.20/piece
Details as per the samples dispatched by the seller on April 21, 2011.		

Total Amount: USD124,342.00

Trade Terms: CIF Kobe

Packing: 538A: 100pcs/ctn, 150ctns/20'FCL
538B: 50pcs/ctn, 150ctns/20'FCL

Delivery Time: By the end of June 2011 without partial shipments

Insurance: Covering for 110% CIF value against All Risks and War Risk

Payment Terms: L/C at sight

For and on behalf of
Kaneyoshi Co., Ltd.

Ayumi Hamasaki
General Manager

天津天宝服装进出口有限公司
Tianjin Tianbao Garment I/E Co., Ltd

27th-Apr-2011

Mr. Genichiro Sata
Kaneyoshi Co., Ltd.
14-22 Kyomachi-Bori 2-Chome
Nishi-Ku, Kobe, JAPAN

Dear Mr. Sata,

We are pleased to receive your mail of April 26th and your order No. KANT-11-0426.

We noted the ordered quantity for Article No.538B, 4960 pieces, cannot satisfy the packing mode, which is 50 pieces/ctn. Therefore we suggest adjusting the quantity to 4950 pieces.

We have enclosed our Sales Confirmation No.TE11PT005, in anticipating of your acceptance, and if there is no objection, please countersign it and return one copy for our file.

In order to help us to meet the date of delivery, please open the relevant letter of credit accordingly.

You may rest assured that we shall make up your order upon receipt of the credit and effect the shipment in June.

If there is any further information you require, please feel free to contact us. Thank you very much for your order, and we look forward to hearing from you again soon.

Yours sincerely,
Tianjin Tianbao Garment I/E Co., Ltd

Deng Xin

中国天津和平区岳阳道 66 号
No.66 Yueyang Road, Heping District, Tianjin 300140, China
电话/Tel:86-22-58818844   传真/Fax:86-22-58818766   网址/Web: www.Tianbao.com.cn

Tianjin Tianbao Garment I/E Co., Ltd.
No.66 Yueyang Road, Heping District,
Tianjin 300140, China
Tel:86-22-58818844
Fax:86-22-58818766

SALES CONFIRMATION

S/C No.: TE11PT005
S/C Date: April 27th, 2011

To: Kaneyoshi Co., Ltd.
14-22 Kyomachi-Bori 2-Chome
Nishi-Ku, Kobe, JAPAN

We hereby confirm having sold to you the following goods on terms and conditions as specified below:

Article No.	Name of Commodity & Specifications	Quantity	Unit Price	Amount
	Men's Pajamas			CIF Kobe
	details as per the samples dispatched by the seller on April 21, 2011 INCOTERMS® 2010			
538A	Men's Pajama Trousers (100% cotton)	21900 pieces	USD4.50	USD98,550.00
538B	Men's Night Shirts (100% cotton)	4950 pieces	USD5.20	USD25,740.00
	Total:	26850 pieces		USD124,290.00

Total Amount in Words: Say U.S. Dollars One Hundred and Twenty Four Thousand Two Hundred and Ninety Only.

Packing: 38A: 100pcs/ctn, 150ctns/20'FCL
538B: 50pcs/ctn, 150ctns/20'FCL
Total 318 cartons in Two 20' FCL.
Shipment: To be effected during June 2011 from Tianjin Xingang, China to Kobe, Japan.
Insurance: To be covered by the seller for 110% of invoice value against all risks and war risk as per the Ocean Marine Cargo Clauses of PICC dated Jan.1, 1981.
Payment: The buyer should open through a bank acceptable to the seller an irrevocable letter of credit payable at sight for 100% of the contract value to reach the seller by the end of May 2011 and valid for negotiation in China until the 10th day after the date of shipment.

Confirmed by:

THE SELLER   THE BUYER
Tianjin Tianbao Garment I/E Co., Ltd

（signature）   （signature）

REMARKS:

1. The Buyer shall have the covering letter of credit reach the Seller 45 days before shipment, failing which the Seller reserves the right to rescind without further notice, or to regard as still valid whole or any part of this contract not fulfilled by the Buyer, or to lodge a claim for losses thus sustained, if any.

2. In case of any discrepancy in quality, claim should be filed by the Buyer within 30 days after the arrival of the goods at port of destination; while for quantity discrepancy, claim should be filed by the Buyer within 15 days after the arrival of the goods at port of destination.

3. For transactions concluded on CIF basis, it is understood that the insurance amount will be for 110% of the invoice value against the risks specified in the Sales confirmation. If additional insurance amount or coverage required, the Buyer must have the consent of the Seller before shipment, and the additional premium is to be borne by the Buyer.

4. The Seller shall not hold liable for non-delivery or delay in delivery of the entire lot or a portion of the goods hereunder by reason of natural disasters, war or other causes of Force Majeure. However, the Seller shall notify the buyer as soon as possible and furnish the Buyer within 15 days by registered airmail with a certificate issued by the China Council for the Promotion of International Trade attesting such event(s).

5. All disputes arising out of the performance of, or relating to this contract, shall be settled through negotiation. In case no settlement can be reached through negotiation, the case shall then be submitted to the China International Economic and Trade Arbitration Commission for arbitration in accordance with its arbitral rules. The arbitration shall take place in Tianjin. The arbitral award is final and binding upon both parties.

6. The buyer is requested to sign and return one copy of this contract immediately after receipt of the same. Objection, if any, should be raised by the Buyer within 3 working days, otherwise it is understood that the Buyer has accepted the terms and conditions of this contract.

7. Special conditions: (These shall prevail over all printed terms in case of any conflict.)

2. 开信用证

买方填写开证申请书，提交保证金或抵押品，支付开证手续费，请开证行开立信用证。

进口商在填写开证申请书时应遵循以下原则：①信用证的指示应完整、准确，避免使用模棱两可的语句。②信用证的指示不能违反买卖合同的条款和条件。③信用证的指示不宜将买卖合同内容细化。④信用证的指示应符合UCP600的规定。⑤所有要求的单据种类、形式应以可取得所需货物和确保开证行的债权为原则。

（1）Kaneyoshi公司于5月2日递交申请开证申请函（第28页）和开证申请书（第29、30页），向The Minato Bank Ltd. 申请开证。信用证为不可撤销信用证，以天宝公司为受益人。

（2）2011年5月4日，天宝公司收到中国银行天津分行的信用证通知书（第31页）和The Minato Bank Ltd. 银行开立的信用证（第32、33、34页）。

Kaneyoshi Co., Ltd.
14-22 Kyomachi-Bori 2-Chome
Nishi-Ku, Kobe, JAPAN
Tel: 06-6441-3325
Fax: 06-6445-2391

May 2nd, 2011

Dear Sirs,

We enclose an application form for documentary credit and shall be glad if you will arrange to open for our account an irrevocable letter of credit for USD124,290.00 in favor of the Tianjin Tianbao Garment I/E Co., Ltd., the credit to be valid until June 15th.

The credit which evidence shipment of 26850 pieces of men's pajamas may be used against presentation of the following documents: Bill of Lading, Commercial Invoice, Packing List, Insurance Policy, Certificate of Origin, etc.(details as per the application form). The company may draw on you at 30 days for the shipment.

Yours truly,
Kaneyoshi Co., Ltd.
Genichiro Sata
Genichiro Sata

IRREVOCABLE DOCUMENTARY CREDIT APPLICATION

TO: THE MINATO BANK LTD.　　　　　　　Date: May 2nd, 2011

Beneficiary (full name and address) TIANJIN TIANBAO GARMENT I/E CO., LTD. NO. 66 YUEYANG ROAD, HEPING DISTRICT TIANJIN 300140, CHINA		L/C No. Ex – Card No. Contract No.: TE11PT005
Partial shipments ☒allowed ☐not allowed	Transshipment ☐allowed ☒not allowed	Date and place of expiry of the credit June 30th, 2011 JAPAN
Loading on board/dispatch/taking in charge at/from XINGANG, CHINA Not later than June 20th, 2011 For transportation to KOBE, JAPAN		☐Issue by airmail (with brief advice by teletransmission) ☐Issue by express delivery ☒Issue by teletransmission (which shall be the operative instrument)
Description of goods: 2 ITEMS OF TOTAL 26850 PIECES OF MEN'S PAJAMAS SPECIFICATIONS AND PACKING CONDITIONS ARE AS PER ATTACHMENT TO THIS APPLICATION		Amount (both in figures and words) USD124,290.00 (SAY U.S. DOLLARS ONE HUNDRED AND TWENTY FOUR THOUSAND TWO HUNDRED AND NINETY ONLY)
Credit available with ☐by sight payment ☐by acceptance ☐by negotiation ☐by deferred payment at against the documents detailed herein ☒and beneficiary's draft for 100% of the invoice value at 30 days after sight on THE MINATO BANK LTD. KOBE, JAPAN		☐FOB ☐CFR ☒CIF ☐or other terms

Documents required: (marked with x)
1. (X) Signed Commercial Invoice in 1 original and 2 copies made out in the name of applicant indicating CREDIT NO.
2. (X) Full set of clean on board ocean Bills of Lading made out to order and blank endorsed, marked "freight ( ) to collect/(X) prepaid ( ) showing freight amount" notifying the applicant.
3. ( ) Air Waybills showing: "freight ( ) to collect/ ( ) prepaid ( ) indicating freight amount" and consigned to ____
____.
4. ( ) Memorandum issued by consigned to.
5. (X) Insurance Policy/Certificate in 3 copies for 120% of the invoice value showing claims payable in Japan in currency of the draft, blank endorsed, covering (X) Ocean Marine Transportation/ ( ) Air Transportation/ ( ) Over Land Transportation Institute Cargo Clauses (A) and Institute War Clauses – Cargo.

6. (X) Packing List in 1 original and 2 copies mentioning total number of packages, gross weight and measurements of each package and packing conditions as called for by the L/C.

7. (　) Certificate of Quantity/weight in 2 copies issued by an independent surveyor at the loading port, indicating the actual surveyed quantity/weight of shipped goods as well as the packing condition.

8. (　) Certificate of Quality in copies issued by [　] manufacturer/ [　] public recognized surveyor or/ [　] beneficiary.

9. (　) Beneficiary's certified copy of cable/telex dispatched to the accountee within 2 working days after shipment advising [　] name of vessel/ [　] air flight No. / [　] wagon No., [　] date, shipping marks, numbers of LC, B/L, contract and order as well as quantity, weight and value of shipment.

10. (X) Beneficiary's certificate stating that shipping documents including invoice, packing list, B/L copy have been sent by fax to applicant (Fax: 06 - 6445 - 2391) after shipment.

11. (X) Other documents, if any:

a. Copy of certificate of origin in duplicate stating that the goods are of Chinese origin.

b. Original and copy of quality inspection certificate issued and signed by the applicant.

c. Original and copy of quality inspection certificate issued and signed by the applicant.

Additional instructions:

1. (　) All banking charges outside the opening bank are for beneficiary's account.

2. (X) Documents must be presented with 10 days after the date of issuance of the transport documents but within the validity of this credit.

3. (　) Third party as shipper is not acceptable. Short Form/Blank Back B/L is not acceptable.

4. (　) Both quantity and amount 10% more or less are allowed.

5. (　) prepaid freight drawn in excess of L/C amount is acceptable against presentation of original charges voucher issued by Shipping Co. /Air line/or it's agent.

6. (X) All documents to be forwarded in one cover, unless otherwise stated above.

(X) Other terms, if any:

All banking charges including opening fee are for beneficiary's account.

You correspondents to advise beneficiary☐adding their confirmation ☐without adding their confirmation

Payments to be debited to our account no 9678999 _____

pre pro KANEYOSHI CO., LTD.

(sgd.)

Genichiro sata

Genichiro sata

TIANJIN BRANCH

信 用 证 通 知 书
Notification of Documentary Credit

ADDRESS:26 NANJING ROAD
TELEX:45089 BOCTJ CN
SWIFT: BKCHCNBJ200

To: 致:	WHEN CORRESPONDING PLEASE QUOTE OUR REF. NO.	YEAR-MONTH-DAY
TIANJIN TIANBAO GARMENT I/E CO., LTD. NO.66 YUEYANG ROAD, HEPING DISTRICT TIANJIN 300140, CHINA		BP70221563
		2011-05-04
Issuing Bank 开证行 THE MINATO BANK LTD. KOBE, JAPAN	**Transmitted to us through** 转递行/转让行	
L/C No. 信用证号 866-10-014759	Dated 开证日期 2011-05-04	Amount 金额 USD124,290.00

Dear Sirs, 径启者

We advise you that we have received from the a/m bank a(n) letter of credit, content of which are as per attached sheet(s).
兹通知贵公司,我行收自上述银行信用证一份,现随附通知。
This advice and attached sheet(s) must accompany the relative documents when presented for negotiation.
贵司交单时,请将本通知书及信用证一并提示。
This advice does not convey any engagement or obligation on our part unless we have added our confirmation.
本通知书不构成我行对此信用证的任何责任和义务,但我行对本证加具保兑的除外。
If you find any terms and conditions in the L/C which you are unable to comply with and/or any error(s), it is suggested that you contact applicant directly for necessary amendment(s) so as to avoid any difficulties which may arise when documents are presented.
如本证中有无法办到的条款及/或错误,请径与开证申请人联系,进行必要的修改,以排除交单时可能发生的问题。
THIS L/C ADVISED SUBJECT TO ICC UCP PUBLICATION NO.600.
本证之通知系遵循国际商会跟单信用证统一惯例第 600 号出版物办理。

This L/C consists of   FOUR   sheet(s), including the covering letter and attachment(s).
本信用证连同面函及附件共   4   页。

Remarks: 备注:
感谢您选择中行,我们将竭诚服务
我行总机电话:38824588   传真:50372594
信用证通知查询电话:22111, 22108 分机
信用证转让咨询:22106 分机
敬请垂询我行下列贸易融资服务:
福费廷(包买票据)和保理业务: 22046, 22047 分机
出口押汇业务:22028, 22030, 22057 分机
也可就近向我们各个支行的国际结算科查询

Yours faithfully,
For BANK OF CHINA

Eximbills Enerpriste Incoming Swift
:::
Message Type: MT700
Send Bank: HSINJPJKXXX

Recv Bank: BKCHCNBJ200

User Name: tj101056
Print Times :2
Print Date: 2011-05-04 MIR : 110125HSINJPJKAXXX5471410605
:::
: 27: [Sequence of Total]
1/1
: 40A: [Form of Documentary Credit]
IRREVOCABLE
: 20: [Documentary Credit Number]
866-10-014759
: 31C: [Date of Issue]
110504
: 40E: [Applicable Rules]
UCP LATEST VERSION
: 31D: [Date and Place of Expiry]
110630 JAPAN
: 50: [Applicant]
KANEYOSHI CO., LTD.
14-22, KYOMACHI-BORI, 2-CHOME,
NISHI-KU, KOBE, JAPAN
: 59: [Beneficiary]
TIANJIN TIANBAO GARMENT I/E CO., LTD.
NO.66 YUYANG ROAD HEPING DISTRICT,
TIANJIN, CHINA
: 32B: [Currency Code, Amount]
USD124,290.00
: 39A: [Percentage Credit Amount Tolerance]
05/05
: 41D: [Available With … By …]
ANY BANK
BY NEGOTIATION
: 42C: [Drafts at …]
DRAFTS AT 30 DAYS AFTER SIGHT FOR FULL INVOICE VALUE
: 42A: [Drawee]
THE MINATO BANK LTD.
KOBE, JAPAN
: 43P: [Partial Shipments]
ALLOWED

: 43T: [Transshipment]
PROHIBITED
: 44E: [Port of Loading/ Airport of Departure]
XINGANG, CHINA
: 44F: [Port of Discharge/ Airport of Destination]
KOBE, JAPAN
: 44C: [Latest Date of Shipment]
110620
: 45A: [Description of Goods and/or Services]
+ CONT NO. AMOUNT (USD)
(1) 21,900PCS OF MEN'S PAJAMA TROUSERS, TE11PT005   98,550.00
(2) 4,960PCS OF MEN'S NIGHT SHIRTS, TE11PT005   25,740.00
TOTAL AMOUNT USD124, 290.00
CIF KOBE, JAPAN
: 46A: [Documents Required]
+SIGNED COMMERCIAL INVOICE IN TRIPLICATE INDICATING CREDIT NO.
+FULL SET OF ORIGINAL CLEAN ON BOARD OCEAN B/L, MADE OUT TO ORDER AND BLANK ENDORSED, MARKED "FREIGHT PREPAID" AND NOTIFY APPLICANT
(TEL: 06-6441-3325 FAX 06-6445-2391)
+PACKING LIST IN TRIPLICATE MENTIONING TOTAL NUMBER OF PACKAGES, GROSS WEIGHT, AND MEASUREMENTS OF EACH PACKAGE.
+BENEFICIARY'S CERTIFICATE STATING THAT ONE SET OF NON-NEGOTIABLE SHIPPING DOCUMENTS INCLUDING INVOICE, PACKING LIST, B/L HAVE BEEN SENT BY FAX TO APPLICANT (FAX 06-6445-2391) AFTER SHIPMENT.
+FULL SET 3/3 OF MARINE INSURANCE POLICY OR CERTIFICATE, ENDORSED IN BLANK FOR 120 PERCENT OF FULL CIF VALUE, COVERING INSTITUTE CARGO CLAUSES(A) AND INSTITUTE WAR CLAUSES-CARGO, SHOWING CLAIMS PAYABLE IN JAPAN.
+ORIGINAL CERTIFICATE OF ORIGIN STATING THAT THE GOODS ARE OF CHINESE ORIGIN.
+ORIGINAL QUALITY INSPECTION CERTIFICATE IN DUPLICATE ISSUED AND SIGNED BY THE APPLICANT.
: 47A: [Additional Conditions]
+5PCT. MORE OF LESS IN QUANTITY AND AMOUNT ARE ALLOWED.
+T.T. REIMBURSEMENT IS NOT ACCEPTABLE
+REIMBURSEMENT IS SUBJECT TO ICC URR725
+IF THE DOCUMENTS ARE PRESENTED WITH DISCREPANCY (IES),
THE DISCREPANCY FEE OF JPY5, 000. (USD50.00 EUR40.00 OR EQUIVALENT) SHOULD BE DEDUCTED FROM YOUR REIMBURSEMENT CLAIM TO THE REIMBURSING BANK OR WILL BE DEDUCTED FROM PROCEEDS BY US, ANY CHARGES RELATED TO ADVICE OF DISCREPANCY (IES), ACCEPTANCE AND/OR PAYMENT ARE FOR ACCOUNT OF BENEFICIARY.
: 71B: [Charges]
+ ALL BANKING CHARGES INCLUDING OPENING FEE ARE FOR BENEFICIARY'S ACCOUNT.

```
: 48: [Period for Presentation]
DOCUMENTS TO BE PRESENTED WITHIN 10 DAYS AFTER THE DATE OF
SHIPMENT BUT WITHIN THE VALIDITY OF THE CREDIT.
: 49: [Confirmation Instructions]
WITHOUT
: 53A: [Reimbursing Bank]
IRVTRUS3NRMB
: 78: [Instructions to the Paying/Accepting/Negotiating Bank]
+YOU MAY REIMBURSE YOURSELVES TO THE REIMBURSEMENT BANK (BANK
OF NEW YORK MELLON, NEW YORK ATTN: REIMBURSEMENT DEPARTMENT
6023 AIRPORT ROAD ORISKANY, N.Y.13424) AND MUST SEND ALL DOCUMENTS
DIRECTLY TO THE MINATO BANK LTD.,INT'L DEPT., 2-1-1, SANNOMIYA-CHO,
CHUO-KU,KOBE, 651-0193 JAPAN BY COURIER IN ONE LOT.
+++ BANK TO BANK INFORMATION ONLY +++
+IN CASE OF REMITTANCE, JPY4, 000. (OR USD35.00 OR EQUIVALENT) WILL BE
DEDUCTED FROM THE PROCEEDS FOR EACH SETTLEMENT OF DOCS.
+IN CASE OF CABLE AUTHORIZATION REQUIRED, USD30.00 (OR EQUIVALENT)
WILL BE DEDUCTED FROM THE PROCEEDS
+PLS COLLECT YOUR ADVISING FEE BEFORE YOU DELIVER THE ORIGINAL L/C
TO BENEFICIARY
: 57D: ["Advise through" Bank]
BANK OF CHINA TIANJIN BRANCH
26, NANJING ROAD, HEXI DISTRICT,
TIANJIN, CHINA
SWIFT: BKCHCNBJ200
-}{5: {MAC: 9B262D90} {CHK:721A2BE1FA4E}}
```

3. 审核与修改信用证

出口商收到买方开来的信用证后，要以合同为依据审核信用证。如有增加出口商成本或业务风险的条款，可要求买方修改信用证。

双方达成的合同是出口商审核信用证的主要依据，此外还要考虑国内的有关政策和规定、国际商会600号出版物即《跟单信用证统一惯例》（UCP600），以及实际业务操作中出现的具体情况。

信用证的审核主要有以下要点：

（1）对信用证本身的审核，包括：

① 是否适用UCP600，开证行资信状况，信用证的付款保证。

② 银行费用：如未事先商定，应由双方共同承担，一般情况下，发生在开证行的所有费用应由进口商负担，而开证行所在国以外的费用通常会规定由出口商负担。

③ 兑付方式、到期日、到期地点、交单期限，应与合同规定一致，一般到期地点应在出口国。

④ 信用证金额、币种、付款期限规定是否与合同的支付条款一致。

（2）申请人和受益人是否与合同相符。

(3) 商品品名、货号、规格、数量、包装规定特别是贸易术语是否与合同一致。如果合同有溢短装条款，则应在信用证的金额和数量上均有相应体现。

(4) 逐项审核单据要求，注意所要求提供的单据是否与卖方根据合同应履行的义务一致，是否给受益人带来额外的风险或费用支出；另外，还应审核单据的转让和交付要求，是否保证卖方在收到货款之前控制物权。如：①CFR 交易中，要求提交保险单，CIF 提高投保加成的比率。②限制卖方装运，如规定"货物只能待收到申请人指定船名和装运通知后装运，而装运通知将由开证行随后以信用证修改书的方式发出。受益人应将该修改书包括在议付单据中"。③单据的出具权掌握在申请人或其代理人手中，如"有开证申请人或其代表签署的检验证书一份"。④关于物权控制的不合理条款，如"货物装运后正本提单径寄买方，或航空运单以进口商为收货人"等。

在本章案例中，天宝公司业务员经审核来证，发现不符点，致函买方，要求改证。（第 36 页）

2011 年 5 月 10 日，天宝公司接中国银行天津分行通知，收到 The Minato Bank Ltd. 银行开立的信用证修改书，经审核，符合公司的改证要求。（第 37 页）

天津天宝服装进出口有限公司
Tianjin Tianbao Garment I/E Co., Ltd

5 May, 2011

Mr. Genichiro Sata
Kaneyoshi Co., Ltd.
14-22 Kyomachi-Bori 2-Chome
Nishi-Ku, Kobe, JAPAN

Dear Mr. Trooborg,

Thank you for your L/C No.866-10-014759 issued by The Minato Bank Ltd. dated May 4th, 2011. However, we have found the following discrepancies after checking with our S/C No.TE11PT005:

1) 31D Date and place of expiry
   The expiry date should be extended to 110710 as contracted to be 10 days after shipment. The expiry place should be China as contracted, instead of Japan.

2) 59 Beneficiary
   Our address is Yueyang Road, not Yuyang Road.

3) 42C Draft at
   The draft should be paid at sight as contracted, instead of at 30 days after sight.

4) 44C Latest date of shipment
   Latest date of shipment should be 110630 as contracted, instead of 110620.

5) 45A Description of goods and/or services
   The total quantity of Men's Night Shirts should be 4950 pieces instead of 4960 pieces as you have confirmed to adjust so.

6) 46A Documents required
   +Please amend "original quality inspection certificate in duplicate issued and signed by the applicant "to" quality inspection certificate in duplicate issued by public recognized surveyor".
   +We have also noticed that you increased the insurance amount to 120% of full CIF value instead of 110%. This will incur the additional premium, which is contracted to be borne by you. Please confirm the change.

7) 71B Charges
   The opening fee is to be borne by applicant according to the usual practices. So please amend to "All banking charges outside Japan are for beneficiary's account".

Please let us have the L/C amendment soon so that we can effect shipment within the contracted time.

Yours sincerely,
Tianjin Tianbao Garment I/E Co., Ltd.

Deng Xin

中国天津和平区岳阳道66号
No.66 Yueyang Road, Heping District, Tianjin 300140, China
电话/Tel:86-22-58818844   传真/Fax:86-22-58818766   网址/Web: www.Tianbao.com.cn

Eximbills Enerpriste Incoming Swift

Message Type: MT700
Send Bank: HSINJPJKXXX

Recv Bank: BKCHCNBJ200

User Name: tj101056
Print Times :2
Print Date: 2011-05-10 MIR : 110125HSINJPJKAXXX5471410605

SENDER'S REFERENCE   *20 : 866 10 014759
RECEIVER'S REFERENCE   *21 : NONREF
NUMBER OF AMENDMENT   26E : 1
DATE OF AMENDMENT   30 : 110510
DATE OF ISSUE   31C :110504

BENEFICIARY (BEFORE THIS AMENDMENT)   *59:
TIANJIN TIANBAO GARMENT I/E CO., LTD.
NO.66 YU YANG ROAD, HEPING DISTRICT
TIANJIN 300140, CHINA

NARRATIVE   79 :
++ UNDER FIELD 31D
   AMEND "110630   JAPAN " TO "110710   CHINA"
++ UNDER FIELD 59
   AMEND "YUYANG ROAD" TO "YUEYANG ROAD"
++ UNDER FIELD 42C
   AMEND TO READ: DRAFT AT SIGHT FOR FULL INVOICE VALUE
++ UNDER FIELD 44C
   AMEND TO READ: 110630
++ UNDER FIELD 45A
   AMEND "4960 PIECES" TO "4950 PIECES"
++ UNDER FIELD 46A
   AMEND "FULL SET 3/3 OF MARINE INSURANCE POLICY...FOR 120 PERCENT OF FULL CIF VALUE…" TO "FULL SET 3/3 OF MARINE INSURANCE POLICY...FOR 110 PERCENT OF FULL CIF VALUE…"
++ UNDER FIELD 46A
   DELETE THE CLAUSE "ORIGINAL QUALITY INSPECTION CERTIFICATE IN DUPLICATE ISSUED AND SIGNED BY THE APPLICANT" AND ADD THE CLAUSE "ORIGINAL QUALITY INSPECTION CERTIFICATE IN DUPLICATE ISSUED AND SIGNED BY PUBLIC RECOGNIZED SURVEYOR"
++ UNDER FIELD 71B
   AMEND TO READ:
   ALL BANKING CHARGES OUTSIDE JAPAN ARE FOR BENEFICIARY'S ACCOUNT
ALL OTHER TERMS AND CONDITIONS REMAIN UNCHANGED

SEND TO REC. INFO.   72 : /PHONEBEN/
TAILER   <MAC:9KE93827> <CHK: 6C3E21452S1E>

4. 出口托运

从这个环节开始，在托运、报检、投保、报关、出运等环节，出口商虽然主要与国内的贸易服务企业以及贸易管理部门打交道，但也要时刻牢记信用证与合同的要求，在办理相关业务时，预先控制，使反馈单据与信用证要求一致，确保顺利结汇；在买方付款之前，确保对物权、保险索赔权等的控制。

出口企业一般委托货运代理向船公司订舱，流程如下：①出口公司缮制"出口货物订舱委托书"、商业发票和装箱单，一并交给货运代理，委托其向船公司订舱。②货运代理收到出口商的委托书后，缮制"集装箱货物海运托运单"（俗称"十联单"），向船公司订舱。③船公司接受订舱后，在"十联单"上标注船名、航次和D/R编号，加盖船公司签章并作装船日期批注，然后将"十联单"中第五联至第十联返还给货运代理。④货运代理留存第八联后，将第五、六、七、九、十联交给出口商。

（1）2011年5月25日，天宝公司委托货运代理向船公司订舱。天宝公司向货代提交的出口托运单据有出口货物订舱委托书（第39页）、装箱单（第40页）、商业发票（第41页）。

（2）2011年5月28日，天宝公司从货运代理处收到订舱确认的反馈文件，即"十联单"中的第五、六、七、九、十联。其中，第五联至第七联主要用作日后报关，第九、十联则为"配舱回单"。

第五联，装货单，场站收据副本（SHIPPING ORDER，S/O），又称关单。是船公司或其代理向船上负责人（船长或大副）和集装箱装卸作业区签发的一种通知其接受装货的指示文件。装货单是报关时必须向海关提交的单据之一；海关查验后，在装货单上加盖放行章，托运人才能凭此装货单要求装货。这也是装货单习称关单的缘由。（第42页）

第六联，场站收据副本，大副联。供港区配载使用，由港区或大副留存。（第43页）

第七联，场站收据（Dock Receipt，D/R）。是指承运人委托集装箱堆场、集装箱货运站或内陆站在收到整箱货或拼箱货后签发的收据。场站收据的作用类似于传统运输（件杂货、散货运输）中的大副收据（Mate's Receipt，M/R），托运人可凭经签收的D/R向船公司或其代理换取正本提单。（第44页）

第九联，配舱回单上有与提单号码一致的D/R编号、承运船名、航次、装船日期，还有船公司的签单章（也有船公司仅盖在第五联装货单上），即表示船公司已确认了发货人的订舱。（第45页）

天津天宝服装进出口有限公司
Tianjin Tianbao Garment I/E Co., Ltd

出口货物订舱委托书

日期 2011/05/25

发货人		
TIANJIN TIANBAO GARMENT I/E CO., LTD. NO.66 YUEYANG ROAD, HEPING DISTRICT TIANJIN 300140, CHINA	装船期限	JUNE 30, 2011
	运输方式	☑ BY SEA ☐ BY AIR
	装箱方式	☑ FCL ☐ LCL
	集装箱种类	☑ 20'GP ☐ 40'GP
	集装箱数量	2
收货人	转船运输	☐ YES ☑ NO
TO ORDER	分批装运	☑ YES ☐ NO
	运费交付	☑ PREPAID ☐ COLLECT
被通知人	装运口岸	XINGANG
KANEYOSHI CO., LTD. 14-22 KYOMACHI-BORI 2-CHOME NISHI-KU, KOBE, JAPAN TEL:06-6441-3325	目的港	KOBE
	成交条件	CIF
	联系人	邓鑫
	电传/传真	022- 58818844

标记唛码	货物描述	总件数	总毛重	总尺码
AS PER INVOICE NO. TE11PT005	MEN'S PAJAMAS (100% COTTON)	318CTNS	3155.000KGS	49.646M³

备注 1) 提单须标明 "FREIGHT PREPAID"

中国天津和平区岳阳道66号
No.66 Yueyang Road, Heping District, Tianjin 300140, China
电话/Tel:86-22-58818844 传真/Fax:86-22-58818766 网址/Web: www.Tianbao.com.cn

Tianjin Tianbao Garment I/E Co., Ltd.
No.66 Yueyang Road, Heping District
Tianjin 300140, China
Tel: 86-22-58818844
Fax:86-22-58818766

PACKING LIST

TO: KANEYOSHI CO., LTD.　　　　　　　　　　INV.NO.:　01TE11PT005
　　　14-22 KYOMACHI-BORI 2-CHOME　　　　INV. DATE: MAY 25, 2011
　　　NISHI-KU, KOBE, JAPAN
FROM:　TIANJIN XINGANG　　TO:　KOBE　　　SHIPPED BY _____

C/ NOS.	DESCRIPTION OF GOODS	PKG	QTY	G.W.	N.W.	MEAS
	MEN'S PAJAMAS (100% COTTON))					
538A TJP2011-04-26 KOBE CARTON NO.1-219 MADE IN CHINA	538A	219CTNS	21900PCS	2103.000KGS	1445.000KGS	33.646M³
538B TJP2011-04-26 KOBE CARTON NO.1-99 MADE IN CHINA	538B	99CTNS	4950PCS	1052.000KGS	715.360KGS	16.000 M³
	TOTAL:	318CTNS	26850 PCS	3155.000KGS	2160.360KGS	49.646M³

TOTAL PACKAGES IN WORDS:　SAY THREE HUNDRED AND EIGHTEEN CARTONS ONLY

MARKS & NOS.: AS SHOWN IN C/NO.

天津天宝服装进出口有限公司
TIANJIN TIANBAO GARMENT I/E CO., LTD.

_____
(SIGNATURE)

Tianjin Tianbao Garment I/E Co., Ltd.
No.66 Yueyang Road, Heping District
Tianjin 300140, China
Tel: 86-22-58818844
Fax:86-22-58818766

COMMERCIAL INVOICE

TO: KANEYOSHI CO., LTD. 　　　　　　　　　INV.NO.: 01TE11PT005
　　14-22 KYOMACHI-BORI 2-CHOME　　　　 INV. DATE: MAY 25, 2011
　　NISHI-KU, KOBE, JAPAN　　　　　　　　　S/C NO.: TE11PT005
FROM: TIANJIN XINGANG　　TO: KOBE　　　SHIPPED BY _____

MARKS & NOS.	DESCRIPTION OF GOODS	QUANTITY	UNIT PRICE	AMOUNT
538A TJP2011-04-26 KOBE CARTON NO. 1-219 MADE IN CHINA	MEN'S PAJAMAS (100% COTTON) 538A　MEN'S PAJAMA TROUSERS 538B　MEN'S NIGHT SHIRTS	 21900PCS 4950PCS	CIF KOBE USD4.50 USD5.20	 USD98,550.00 USD25,740.00 USD124,290.00
538B TJP2011-04-26 KOBE CARTON NO.1-99 MADE IN CHINA				

　　　　　　　　　TOTAL AMOUNT IN WORDS: SAY U.S. DOLLARS ONE HUNDRED AND TWENTY FOUR
　　　　　　　　　　　　　　　　　　　　　THOUSAND TWO HUNDRED AND NINETY ONLY.
　　　　　　　　　TOTAL G.W./TOTAL N.W.: 3155.000KGS/2160.360KGS
　　　　　　　　　TOTAL PACKAGES:　　　 318CTNS

　　　　　　　　　　　　　　　天津天宝服装进出口有限公司
　　　　　　　　　　　　　　　TIANJIN TIANBAO GARMENT I/E CO., LTD.

　　　　　　　　　　　　　　　　　_____
　　　　　　　　　　　　　　　　　　　　(SIGNATURE)

Shipper(发货人)	D/R NO.(编号)	
TIANJIN TIANBAO GARMENT I/E CO., LTD. NO.66 YUEYANG ROAD, HEPING DISTRICT TIANJIN 300140, CHINA	COSU89302173	
Consignee(收货人) TO ORDER	装 货 单	第五联
Notify Party (通知人) KANEYOSHI CO., LTD. 14-22 KYOMACHI-BORI 2-CHOME NISHI-KU, KOBE, JAPAN TEL: 06-6441-3325	Received by the Carrier the Total number of containers or other packages or units stated below to be transported subject to the terms and conditions of the Carrier's regular form of Bill of Lading (for Combined Transport or port to port shipment) which shall be deemed to be incorporated herein.	
Pre-carriage by(前程运输)	Place of Receipt(收货地点)	
Vessel(船名) Voy. No.(航次) COSCO HELLAS / 013W	Port of loading(装货港) XINGANG	Date(日期): May 28, 2011 场站章
Port of Discharge(卸货港) KOBE	Place of delivery(交货地点)	Final Destination for the Merchant's Reference (目的地)

Container No. (集装箱号)	Seal No.(封志号) Marks & Nos. (标志与号码)	No. of containers or pkgs (箱数或件数)	Kind of Packages: Description of Goods (包装种类与货名)	Gross Weight 毛重(公斤)	Measurement 尺码(立方米)
	538A TJP2011-04-26 KOBE CARTON NO.1-219 MADE IN CHINA	318CNTS	MEN'S PAJAMAS	3155.000KGS	49.646CBM
	538B TJP2011-04-26 KOBE CARTON NO.1-99 MADE IN CHINA		FREIGHT PREPAID		

Particulars Furnished by Merchants (托运人提供详细情况)

TOTAL NUMBER OF CONTAINERS OR PACKAGES (IN WORDS) 集装箱数或件数合计(大写)   SAY THREE HUNDRED AND EIGHTEEN CARTONS ONLY

Container No.(箱号)	Seal No.(封志号)	Pkgs.(件数)	Container No.(箱号)	Seal No.(封志号)	Pkgs.(件数)

Received(实收)   By Terminal Clerk(场站员签字)

FREIGHT & CHARGES	Prepaid at (预付地点)	Payable at (到付地点)	Place of Issue (签发地点) TIANJIN
	Total Prepaid (预付总额)	No. of Original B(s)/L (正本提单份数) THREE	Booking (订舱确认) APPROVED BY

Service Type on Receiving ☑ CY ☐ CFS ☐ DOOR	Service Type on Delivery ☑ CY ☐ CFS ☐ DOOR	Reefer Temperature Required(冷藏温度) °F °C 签单章
TYPE OF GOODS (种类)	☑ Ordinary (普通) ☐ Reefer (冷藏) ☐ Dangerous (危险品) ☐ Auto (裸装车辆) ☐ Liquid (液体) ☐ Live Animal (活动物) ☐ Bulk (散装)	危险品 Class: Property: IMDG Code Page: UN No.

Shipper(发货人)		D/R NO.(编号)	
TIANJIN TIANBAO GARMENT I/E CO., LTD. NO.66 YUEYANG ROAD, HEPING DISTRICT TIANJIN 300140, CHINA		COSU89302173	
Consignee(收货人) TO ORDER		场站收据副本 大副联 COPY OF DOCK RECEIPT (FOR CHIEF OFFICER)	第六联
Notify Party (通知人) KANEYOSHI CO., LTD. 14-22 KYOMACHI-BORI 2-CHOME NISHI-KU, KOBE, JAPAN TEL: 06-6441-3325		Received by the Carrier the Total number of containers or other packages or units stated below to be transported subject to the terms and conditions of the Carrier's regular form of Bill of Lading (for Combined Transport or port to port shipment) which shall be deemed to be incorporated herein.	
Pre-carriage by(前程运输)	Place of Receipt(收货地点)		
Vessel(船名) Voy. No.(航次) COSCO HELLAS / 013W	Port of loading(装货港) XINGANG	Date(日期): May 28, 2011	
		场站章	
Port of Discharge(卸货港) KOBE	Place of delivery(交货地点)	Final Destination for the Merchant's Reference (目的地)	

Container No. (集装箱号)	Seal No.(封志号) Marks & Nos. (标志与号码)	No. of containers or pkgs (箱数或件数)	Kind of Packages: Description of Goods (包装种类与货名)	Gross Weight 毛重(公斤)	Measurement 尺码(立方米)
	538A TJP2011-04-26 KOBE CARTON NO.1-219 MADE IN CHINA	318CTNS	MEN'S PAJAMAS	3155.000KGS	49.646CBM
	538B TJP2011-04-26 KOBE CARTON NO.1-99 MADE IN CHINA		FREIGHT PREPAID		

-Particulars Furnished by Merchants (托运人提供详细情况)

TOTAL NUMBER OF CONTAINERS OR PACKAGES (IN WORDS) 集装箱数或件数合计(大写)   SAY THREE HUNDRED AND EIGHTEEN CARTONS ONLY

Container No.(箱号)	Seal No.(封志号)	Pkgs.(件数)	Container No.(箱号)	Seal No.(封志号)	Pkgs.(件数)
			Received(实收)	By Terminal Clerk(场站员签字)	

FREIGHT & CHARGES	Prepaid at (预付地点)	Payable at (到付地点)	Place of Issue (签发地点) TIANJIN
	Total Prepaid(预付总额)	No. of Original B(s)/L (正本提单份数) THREE	Booking (订舱确认) APPROVED BY

Service Type on Receiving ☑ CY ☐ CFS ☐ DOOR	Service Type on Delivery ☑ CY ☐ CFS ☐ DOOR	Reefer temperature Required(冷藏温度) °F °C
TYPE OF GOODS (种类)	☑ Ordinary (普通) ☐ Reefer (冷藏) ☐ Dangerous (危险品) ☐ Auto (裸装车辆) ☐ Liquid (液体) ☐ Live Animal (活动物) ☐ Bulk (散装)	危险品 Class: Property: IMDG Code Page: UN No.

Shipper(发货人)		D/R NO.(编号)	
TIANJIN TIANBAO GARMENT I/E CO., LTD. NO.66 YUEYANG ROAD, HEPING DISTRICT TIANJIN 300140, CHINA		COSU89302173	第七联

Consignee(收货人)	
TO ORDER	**场站收据**
Notify Party (通知人)	**DOCK RECEIPT**
KANEYOSHI CO., LTD. 14-22 KYOMACHI-BORI 2-CHOME NISHI-KU, KOBE, JAPAN TEL: 06-6441-3325	Received by the Carrier the Total number of containers or other packages or units stated below to be transported subject to the terms and conditions of the Carrier's regular form of Bill of Lading (for Combined Transport or port to port shipment) which shall be deemed to be incorporated herein.

Pre-carriage by(前程运输)	Place of Receipt(收货地点)	
Vessel (船名) Voy. No. (航次) COSCO HELLAS / 013W	Port of loading (装货港) XINGANG	Date(日期): May 28, 2011

场站章

Port of Discharge(卸货港) KOBE	Place of delivery(交货地点)	Final Destination for the Merchant's Reference (目的地)

Container No. (集装箱号)	Seal No.(封志号) Marks & Nos. (标志与号码)	No. of containers or pkgs (箱数或件数)	Kind of Packages: Description of Goods (包装种类与货名)	Gross Weight 毛重(公斤)	Measurement 尺码(立方米)
	538A TJP2011-04-26 KOBE CARTON NO.1-219 MADE IN CHINA	318CNTS	MEN'S PAJAMAS	3155.000KGS	49.646CBM
	538B TJP2011-04-26 KOBE CARTON NO.1-99 MADE IN CHINA		FREIGHT PREPAID		

TOTAL NUMBER OF CONTAINERS OR PACKAGES (IN WORDS) 集装箱数或件数合计(大写) — SAY THREE HUNDRED AND EIGHTEEN CARTONS ONLY

Container No.(箱号)	Seal No.(封志号)	Pkgs.(件数)	Container No.(箱号)	Seal No.(封志号)	Pkgs.(件数)

Received(实收)   By Terminal Clerk(场站员签字)

FREIGHT & CHARGES	Prepaid at (预付地点)	Payable at (到付地点)	Place of Issue (签发地点) TIANJIN
	Total Prepaid(预付总额)	No. of Original B(s)/L (正本提单份数) THREE	Booking (订舱确认) APPROVED BY

Service Type on Receiving ☑ CY ☐ CFS ☐ DOOR	Service Type on Delivery ☑ CY ☐ CFS ☐ DOOR	Reefer temperature Required(冷藏温度) °F °C
TYPE OF GOODS (种类) ☑ Ordinary (普通) ☐ Reefer (冷藏) ☐ Dangerous (危险品) ☐ Auto (裸装车辆) ☐ Liquid (液体) ☐ Live Animal (活动物) ☐ Bulk (散装)		危险品 Class: Property: IMDG Code Page: UN No.

Shipper（发货人）			D/R NO.(编号)	
TIANJIN TIANBAO GARMENT I/E CO., LTD. NO.66 YUEYANG ROAD, HEPING DISTRICT TIANJIN 300140, CHINA			COSU89302173	
Consignee(收货人) - TO ORDER			配舱回单（1）	第九联
Notify Party (通知人) KANEYOSHI CO., LTD. 14-22 KYOMACHI-BORI 2-CHOME NISHI-KU, KOBE, JAPAN TEL: 06-6441-3325				
Pre-carriage by(前程运输)		Place of Receipt(收货地点)		
Vessel（船名）Voy. No.（航次） COSCO HELLAS / 013W		Port of loading（装货港） XINGANG		
Port of Discharge(卸货港) KOBE		Place of delivery(交货地点)	Final Destination for the Merchant's Reference (目的地)	
Container No. (集装箱号)	Seal No.(封志号) Marks & Nos. (标志与号码))	No. of containers or pkgs (箱数或件数)	Kind of Packages: Description of Goods (包装种类与货名)	Gross Weight 毛重（公斤）	Measurement 尺码（立方米）
	538A TJP2011-04-26 KOBE CARTON NO.1-219 MADE IN CHINA	318CNTS	MEN'S PAJAMAS	3155.000KGS	49.646CBM
	538B TJP2011-04-26 KOBE CARTON NO.1-99 MADE IN CHINA		FREIGHT PREPAID		

Particulars Furnished by Merchants (托运人提供详细情况)

TOTAL NUMBER OF CONTAINERS OR PACKAGES (IN WORDS) 集装箱数或件数合计(大写)	SAY THREE HUNDRED AND EIGHTEEN CARTONS ONLY		
Container No(箱号)		Seal No.(封志号)	
装船日期：2011年6月12日		Received(实收) By Terminal Clerk (场站员签字)	

FREIGHT & CHARGES	Prepaid at (预付地点)	Payable at (到付地点)	Place of Issue (签发地点) TIANJIN
	Total Prepaid (预付总额)	No. of Original B(s)/L (正本提单份数) THREE	Booking (订舱确认) APPROVED BY
		Reefer temperature Required(冷藏温度)	°F °C

Service Type on Receiving ☑ CY ☐ CFS ☐ DOOR	Service Type on Delivery ☑ CY ☐ CFS ☐ DOOR		
TYPE OF GOODS (种类)	☑ Ordinary (普通) ☐ Reefer (冷藏) ☐ Liquid (液体) ☐ Live Animal (活动物)	☐ Dangerous (危险品) ☐ Auto (裸装车辆) ☐ Bulk (散装)	危险	Class: Property: IMDG Code Page: UN No.

可否转船：NO	可否分批：YES	签单章
装　期：June 30, 2011	效　期：July 10, 2011	(18)
金　额：US$124,290.00		
制单日期：May 28, 2011		

Shipper(发货人) TIANJIN TIANBAO GARMENT I/E CO., LTD. NO.66 YUEYANG ROAD, HEPING DISTRICT TIANJIN 300140, CHINA				D/R NO.(编号) COSU89302173	
Consignee(收货人) - TO ORDER					
Notify Party (通知人) KANEYOSHI CO., LTD. 14-22 KYOMACHI-BORI 2-CHOME NISHI-KU, KOBE, JAPAN TEL: 06-6441-3325				配舱回单（2）	第十联
Pre-carriage by(前程运输)			Place of Receipt(收货地点)		
Vessel（船名）Voy. No.（航次）. COSCO HELLAS / 013W			Port of loading（装货港） XINGANG		
Port of Discharge(卸货港) KOBE			Place of delivery(交货地点)	Final Destination for the Merchant's Reference (目的地)	
Container No. (集装箱号)	Seal No.(封志号) Marks & Nos. （标志与号码））	No. of containers or pkgs （箱数或件数）	Kind of Packages: Description of Goods (包装种类与货名)	Gross Weight 毛重(公斤)	Measurement 尺码(立方米)
	538A TJP2011-04-26 KOBE CARTON NO.1-219 MADE IN CHINA	318CNTS	MEN'S PAJAMAS	3155.000KGS	49.646CBM
	538B TJP2011-04-26 KOBE CARTON NO.1-99 MADE IN CHINA		FREIGHT PREPAID		
TOTAL NUMBER OF CONTAINERS OR PACKAGES (IN WORDS) 集装箱数或件数合计(大写)		SAY THREE HUNDRED AND EIGHTEEN CARTONS ONLY			
Container No(箱号)				Seal No.(封志号)	
		Received(实收) By Terminal Clerk（场站员签字）			
FREIGHT & CHARGES	Prepaid at (预付地点)		Payable at (到付地点)	Place of Issue (签发地点) TIANJIN	
	Total Prepaid (预付总额)		No. of Original B(s)/L （正本提单份数） THREE	Booking（订舱确认） APPROVED BY	
				Reefer temperature Required(冷藏温度)	°F °C
Service Type on Receiving ☑ CY ☐ CFS ☐ DOOR		Service Type on Delivery ☑ CY ☐ CFS ☐ DOOR			
TYPE OF GOODS (种类)	☑ Ordinary (普通) ☐ Liquid (液体)	☐ Reefer (冷藏) ☐ Live Animal (活动物)	☐ Dangerous (危险品) ☐ Bulk (散装)	☐ Auto (裸装车辆)	危险品	Class: Property: IMDG Code Page: UN No.
可否转船: NO		可否分批: YES			
装　期: June 30, 2011		效　期: July 10, 2011			
金　额: US$124,290.00					
制单日期: May 28, 2011					

Particulars Furnished by Merchants (托运人提供详细情况。)

5. 出口货物报检

2011年5月30日，天宝公司向出入境检验检疫局办理出口商品报检手续。

出入境检验检疫是国际贸易不可缺少的环节之一，有国家强制性检验，也有买卖双方自发约定的检验。货物交付之前，若该出口货物是属于国家强制性检验检疫的项目，出口商应依照相关规定，并按一定的程序申请检验检疫，取得出口检验检疫证明方可出口；若该出口货物是买卖合同规定出口商需在出口装运前进行检验检疫的，则由出口商按合同规定，在交付前完成相关检验检疫手续，取得合格证明。

出口货物报检流程如下：①出口商填制"出境货物报检单"，随附商业发票、装箱单，最迟在出口报关前7天向出入境检验检疫机构办理货物出境报检手续。②出入境检验检疫机构受理并收取检验检疫费后，对出口货物实施必要的检验、检疫、消毒等。③出口货物经检验合格后，出入境检验检疫机构对产地与报关地一致的出境货物，向出口商出具"出境货物通关单"和/或商检证书；对产地和报关地不一致的出境货物，则出具"出境货物换证凭单"，出口商凭此单向报关地出入境检验检疫机构换发"出境货物通关单"和/或商检证书。

天宝公司案例中的商品是列入中国《出入境检验检疫机构实施检验检疫的进出境商品目录》中的商品，必须实行法定检验。

天宝公司报检的反馈文件既包括"出境货物通关单"，也包括商检证书。

(1) 2011年5月30日，天宝公司向出入境检验检疫局办理出口商品报检手续，填制出境货物报检单(第48页)，连同商业发票(第41页)、装箱单(第40页)和其他所需材料一起提交给检验机构。

(2) 2011年6月2日，天宝公司收到出入境检验检疫局签发的出境货物通关单(第49页)和品质检验证书(第50页)。

中华人民共和国出入境检验检疫出境货物报检单

报检单位（加盖公章）：天津天宝服装进出口有限公司				*编 号	
报检单位登记号：31009168273	联系人：徐立轩		电话：022-58818844	报检日期：2011年5月30日	

发货人	（中文）天津天宝服装进出口有限公司
	（外文）TIANJIN TIANBAO GARMENT I/E CO., LTD.
收货人	（中文）***
	（外文）KANEYOSHI CO., LTD.

货物名称（中/外文）	H.S.编码	产地	数/重量	货物总值	包装种类及数量
男式睡衣	6207910092	天津市	26850件	124290美元	318纸箱

运输工具名称号码	船舶 COSCO HELLAS/013W	贸易方式	一般贸易	货物存放地点	***
合同号	TE11PT005	信用证号	866-10-014759	用途	***
发货日期	***	输往国家（地区）	日本	许可证/审批号	***
启运地	新港	到达口岸	神户	生产单位注册号	***
集装箱规格数量及号码		2个海运20尺普通箱			

合同、信用证订立的检验检疫条款或特殊要求	标记及号码	随附单据（划"√"或补填）	
	参见发票01TE11PT005	□ 合同 □ 信用证 √ 发票 □ 换证凭证 √ 装箱单	□ 包装性能结果单 □ 许可/审批文件 □ 厂检单

需要单据名称（划"√"或补填）				*检验检疫费	
√ 品质证书	1正1副	□ 植物检疫证书	__正__副	总金额	
□ 重量证书	__正__副	□ 熏蒸/消毒证书	__正__副	（人民币元）	
□ 兽医卫生证书	__正__副	□ 出境货物换证凭单	__正__副	计费人	
□ 健康证书	__正__副	√ 出境货物通关单	1正2副	收费人	
□ 卫生证书	__正__副				
□ 动物卫生证书	__正__副				

报检人郑重声明：
1. 本人被授权报检
2. 上列填写内容正确属实，货物无伪造或冒用他人的厂名、标志、认证标志，并承担货物质量责任。

签名：徐立轩

领取单证	
日期	
签名	

注：有"*"号栏由出入境检验检疫机关填写 ◆国家出入境检验检疫局制
[1-2(2005.1.1)]

中华人民共和国出入境检验检疫

出境货物通关单

编号：120500211005138000

1. 发货人 天津天宝服装进出口有限公司 ***		5. 标记及号码 538A　　　　　　538B TJP2011-04-26　　TJP2011-04-26 KOBE　　　　　　KOBE CARTON NO.1-219　CARTON NO.1-99 MADE IN CHINA　MADE IN CHINA
2. 收货人 ***		
3. 合同/信用证号 TE11PT005/***	4. 输往国家或地区 日本	
6. 运输工具名称及号码 船舶***	7. 发货日期 ***	8. 集装箱规格及数量 2个海运20尺普通箱
9. 货物名称及规格 男式睡衣 *** （以下空白）	10. H.S.编码 6207910092 *** （以下空白）	11. 申报总值 *124290 美元 *** （以下空白）	12. 数/重量、包装数量及种类 *26850 件 *318 纸箱 *** （以下空白）

13. 证明

上述货物业经检验检疫，请海关予以放行。
本通关单有效期至 二〇一一 年 八 月 一 日

签字 刘国栋

日期：2011 年 06 月 02 日

14. 备注
***

【2-2（2000.1.1）】　　①货物通关　　印刷流水号：AA0608243

中华人民共和国出入境检验检疫
ENTRY-EXIT INSPECTION AND QUARANTINE
OF THE PEOPLE'S REPUBLIC OF CHINA

第一页共一页 Page 1 of 1

编号 No. :034909628062673

QUALITY
INSPECTION CERTIFICATE

发货人 Consignor	TIANJIN TIANBAO GARMENT I/E CO., LTD.		
收货人 Consignee	KANEYOSHI CO., LTD.		
品名 Description of Goods	MEN'S PAJAMAS	标记及号码 Mark & No.	
		538A	538B
报检数量/重量 Quantity/Weight Declared	-26850-PCS/-3155-KGS	TJP2011-04-26 KOBE	TJP2011-04-26 KOBE
包装种类及数量 Number and Type of Packages	-318-CTNS	CARTON NO.1-219 MADE IN CHINA	CARTON NO.1-99 MADE IN CHINA
运输工具 Means of Conveyance	COSCO HELLAS/013W		

检验结果:
RESULTS OF INSPECTION:

At the request of consignor, our inspectors attended at the warehouse of the consignment on 2011/05/31. In accordance with SN/T0559-1996, SN/T1649-2005 and the relevant state stipulations GB/T2662-2008 and FZ/T81001-2007, 13 cartons were taken and opened at random for visual inspection, from which representative samples were drawn and inspected according to the stipulation mentioned above. The results are as follows:

Appearance:Pass
Specifications:Pass
Quantity:-26850PCS,-318-CTNS
Safety:Pass
Hygienics:Pass

印章 Official Stamp 签章地点 Place of Issue **TIANJIN**   签证日期 Date of Issue **2 JUNE 2011**

签字人 Authorized Officer **MA MING**   签名 Signature

我们已尽所知和最大能力实施上述检验，不能因我们签发本证书而免除卖方或其他方面根据合同和法律所承担的产品质量责任和其他责任。
All inspections are carried out conscientiously to the best our knowledge and ability. This certificate does not in any respect absolve the seller and other related parties from his contractual and legal obligations especially when product quality is concerned.

B0211476   [c 1-1 (2010.1.1)]

6. 出口货运投保

出口方填制投保单，连同商业发票一起提交给保险公司，并缴纳保险费；保险人承保后签发保险单作为承保的凭证。

如果所保险的货物在运输过程中发生承保风险造成的损失，保险公司应按其出具的保险单的规定给予被保险人经济上的补偿。

CIF 术语下，保险单中的被保险人一般应填写为出口商，信用证结算时即为受益人。这是因为：①根据 Incoterms® 2010 对 CIF 术语买卖双方风险的划分，从货物在指定装运港装上船舶时，其灭失或损坏的风险才由卖方转移至买方（或按 Incoterms® 2000，以装运港船舷为界）。也就是说，在投保时，卖方（而非买方）对即将发运的货物具有保险利益。根据被保险人是保险利益的所有者的原则，保险单上的被保险人应为卖方。②在卖方尚未收妥货款的情况下，以买方作为"被保险人"有较大的风险。一旦碰到买方拒付货款，或是信用证项下出现单证不符而遭到拒付的情况，如果恰遇货物在海运途中发生保险范围内的损失，卖方则无法凭该保险单向保险公司提出索赔。不仅如此，由于保险单据的被保险人是买方，卖方想要转让货物另寻买主也比较困难。所以卖方通常选择将自己作为保险单的被保险人，在向买方交单（或通过银行交单）时，通过在保险单上作必要的背书才将保险利益及索赔权转让给买方。

2011 年 6 月 3 日，天宝公司投保，提交的单据是商业发票（第 41 页）和投保单（第 52 页）。

2011 年 6 月 4 日，天宝公司收到中国人民财产保险股份有限公司天津分公司签发的保险单。（第 53 页）

7. 出口货物原产地认证

在国际贸易中，各国根据各自的对外贸易政策，普遍对进口商品实施差别关税和数量限制，并由海关执行统计，进口国要求出口国出具货物的原产地证明已经成为国际惯例。在各种原产地证明中，一般原产地证明（Certificate of Origin，简称 C/O）和普惠制原产地证明书格式 A（Generalized System of Preferences Certificate of Origin Form A，简称 GSP Form A）是比较常见的两种。

一般原产地证明可由中国国际贸易促进委员会（China Council for the Promotion of International Trade，简称 CCPIT，贸促会）签发，也可由出入境检验检疫局（China Entry – Exit Inspection and Quarantine Bureau）签发。对于普惠制原产地证书，在我国，设在各地的出入境检验检疫局是政府授权的唯一签发机构。

除普惠制原产地证书外，目前商检局可出具的有效的产地证类型还有一般原产地证（C.O），智利原产地证（FORM F），亚太贸易协定原产地证（FORM M），中国—东盟自由贸易区优惠关税原产地证书（FORM E），中国—巴基斯坦自由贸易区原产地证书（FORM P）等。

日本于 1980 年 4 月 1 日起给予我国普惠制待遇。2010 年日本再次削减对华普惠制待遇，从中国进口的产品中，不享受普惠制的产品由 13 种大幅增加到 450 种，产品类别涉及日用品、服装、农产品等，2011 年 4 月 1 日起正式实施。

本案例中日本客户要求出具一般原产地证。

2011 年 6 月 7 日，天宝公司收到由贸促会（CCPIT）签章的一般原产地证明。（第 54 页）

中国人民财产保险股份有限公司 天津市分公司
PICC Property and Casualty Company Limited, Tianjin Branch

地址：中国天津曲阜道78号
ADD: No.78 Qufu Road Tianjin China
邮编（Post Code）：300161

货物运输保险投保单
APPLICATION FORM FOR CARGO TRANSPORTATION INSURANCE

被保险人：
INSURED   TIANJIN TIANBAO GARMENT I/E CO., LTD.
发票号（INVOICE NO.）   01TE11PT005
合同号（CONTRACT NO.）   TE11PT005
信用证号（L/C NO.）   866-10-014759
发票金额（INVOICE AMOUNT）   USD124,290.00   投保加成（PLUS）   10%

兹有下列物品向中国人民财产保险股份有限公司 天津分 公司投保。(INSURANCE IS REQUIRED ON THE FOLLOWING COMMODITIES:)

标记 MARKS & NOS.	包装及数量 QUANTITY	保险货物项目 DESCRIPTION OF GOODS	保险金额 AMOUNT INSURED
AS PER INVOICE NO. 01TE11PT005	318CTNS	MEN'S PAJAMAS	USD136,719.00

启运日期：   装载运输工具：
DATE OF COMMENCEMENT   JUNE 12,2011   PER CONVEYANCE   COSCO HELLAS/013W
自   经   至
FROM   XINGANG   VIA   _____   TO   KOBE
提单号：   赔款偿付地点：
B/L NO.   COSU89302173   CLAIM PAYMENT AT   KOBE

投保险别：(PLEASE INDICATE THE CONDITIONS &/OR SPECIAL COVERAGES)

COVERING INSTITUTE CARGO CLAUSES (A)   AND INSTITUTE WAR CLAUSES-CARGO

备注：(REMARKS)
1) 须三份正本保单

请如实告知下列情况：（如是在[ ]中打 'X'）IF ANY, PLEASE MARK 'X':
1. 货物种类 普通[X]   散装[ ]   冷藏[ ]   液体[ ]   活动物[ ]   机器/汽车[ ]   危险品等级[ ]
   GOODS   ORDINARY   BULK   REEFER   LIQUID   LIVE ANIMAL   MACHINE/AUTO   DANGEROUS CLASS
2. 集装箱种类 普通[X]   开顶[ ]   框架[ ]   平板[ ]   冷藏[ ]
   CONTAINER   ORDINARY   OPEN   FRAME   PLAY   REFERIGERATOR
3. 转运工具   海轮[ ]   飞机[ ]   驳船[ ]   火车[ ]   汽车[ ]
   BY TRANSIT   SHIP   PLANE   BARGE   TRAIN   TRUCK
4. 船舶资料   船籍   船龄
   PARTICULAR OF SHIP   REGISTRY _____   AGE _____

备注：被保险人确认本保险合同条款和内容已经完全了解   投保人（签名盖章）APPLICANT'S SIGNATURE
THE ASSURED CONFIRMS HEREWITH THE TERMS AND
CONDITIONS OF THESE INSURANCE CONTRACT FULLY
UNDERSTOOD.

投保日期：(DATE)   JUNE 3, 2011
电话：(TEL)   022-58818844
地址：(ADD)   NO.66 YUEYANG ROAD,
HEPING DISTRICT
TIANJIN 300140, CHINA

木公司自用（FOR OFFICE USE ONLY）

经办人   核保人   NO.: PICC 1125873
Made By   Checked By

货物运输保险单
CARGO TRANSPORTATION INSURANCE POLICY

PICC 中国人保财险

总公司设于北京　一九四九年创立
Head office Beijing　Established in 1949

发票号（INVOICE NO.）	01TE11PT005	保单号次
合同号（CONTRACT NO.）	TE11PT005	POLICY NO. PYIE201143958015958273
信用证号（L/C NO.）	866-10-014759	
被保险人 INSURED	TIANJIN TIANBAO GARMENT I/E CO., LTD.	

中国人民财产保险股份有限公司（以下简称公司）根据被保险人的要求，由被保险人向本公司交付约定的保险费，按照本保单承保险别和背面所载条款和下列特款承保下述货物运输运输保险，特立本保险单。

THIS POLICY OF INSURANCE WITNESS THAT PICC PROPERTY AND CASUALTY COMPANY LIMITED (HEREINAFTER CALLED "THE COMPANY") AT THE REQUEST OF THE INSURED AND IN CONSIDERATION OF THE AGREED PREMIUM PAID TO THE COMPANY BY THE INSURED, UNDERTAKES TO INSURE THE UNDERMENTIONED GOODS IN TRANSPORTATION SUBJECT TO THE CONDITIONS OF THIS POLICY AS PER THE CLAUSES PRINTED OVERLEAF AND OTHER SPECIAL CLAUSES ATTACHED HEREON.

标记 MARKS & NOS	包装及数量 QUANTITY	保险货物项目 DESCRIPTION OF GOODS	保险金额 AMOUNT INSURED
AS PER INVOICE NO. 01TE11PT005	318CTNS	MEN'S PAJAMAS	USD136,719.00

总保险金额：
TOTAL AMOUNT INSURED: US DOLLARS ONE HUNDRED AND THIRTY SIX THOUSAND SEVEN HUNDRED AND NINETEEN ONLY

保费： PREMIUM AS ARRANGED	启运日期： DATE OF COMMENCEMENT AS PER B/L	装载运输工具： PER CONVEYANCE COSCO HELLAS /013W
自 FROM XINGANG CHINA	经 VIA	至 TO KOBE, JAPAN

承保险别：
CONDITIONS

COVERING INSTITUTE CARGO CLAUSES (A) AND INSTITUTE WAR CLAUSES-CARGO.

所保货物，如发生保险单项下可能引起索赔的损失或损坏，应立即通知本公司下述代理人查勘。 如有索赔，应向本公司提交保单正本（本保单共有 叁 份正本）及有关文件。如一份正本已用于索赔，其余正本自动失效。

IN THE EVENT OF LOSS OR DAMAGE WHICH MAY RESULT IN A CLAIM UNDER THIS POLICY, IMMEDIATE NOTICE MUST BE GIVEN TO THE COMPANY'S AGENT AS MENTIONED HEREUNDER CLAIMS. IF ANY, ONE OF THE ORIGINAL POLICY WHICH HAS BEEN ISSUED IN __3__ ORGINAL(S) TOGETHER WITH THE RELEVENT DOCUMENTS SHALL BE SURRENDERED TO THE COMPANY. IF ONE OF THE ORIGINAL POLICY HAS BEEN ACCOMPLISHED, THE OTHERS TO BE VOID.

3-25 GYOKUSEI-CHO, GIFU-SHI
KOBE, JAPAN
TEL:+06 6441 3678
FAX:+06 6441 3699

中国人民财产保险股份有限公司　天津市分公司
PICC Property and Casualty Company Limited, Tianjin Branch

赔款偿付地点
CLAIM PAYABLE AT/IN　KOBE IN USD
出单日期
ISSUING DATE　JUNE 4,2011

李玉泉
GENERRAL MANAGER

地址：中国天津市曲阜路78号　经办：项军　复核：廖敏　Settling & Customer Service Centre
ADD:78 QUFU ROAD TIANJIN CHINA　　　　（理赔/客户服务中心）86 21 63674274
邮编（POST CODE）：300161　　　　保单顺序号 PICC 1125873

ORIGINAL

1. Exporter TIANJIN TIANBAO GARMENT I/E CO., LTD. NO.66 YUEYANG ROAD, HEPING DISTRICT TIANJIN 300140, CHINA	Certificate No. **CCPIT** 112911238 **CERTIFICATE OF ORIGIN** **OF** **THE PEOPLE'S REPUBLIC OF CHINA**
2. Consignee KANEYOSHI CO., LTD. 14-22 KYOMACHI-BORI 2-CHOME NISHI-KU, KOBE, JAPAN	
3. Means of transport and route (as far as known) FROM XINGANG, CHINA TO KOBE, JAPAN BY SEA	5. For certifying authority use only
4. Country/region of destination JAPAN	

6. Marks and numbers	7. Number and kind of packages; description of goods	8. H.S. Code	9. Quantity	10. Number and date of invoices
538A TJP2011-04-26 KOBE CARTON NO.1-219 MADE IN CHINA 538B TJP2011-04-26 KOBE CARTON NO.1-99 MADE IN CHINA	318 (THREE HUNRED AND EIGHTEEN) CARTONS OF MEN'S PAJAMAS L/C NO: 866-10-014759 ******************************	6207910092	26850 PIECES	01TE11PT005 MAY 25, 2011

11. Declaration by the exporter	12. Certification
The undersigned hereby declares that the above details and statements are correct, that all the goods are produced in China and that they comply with the Rules of Origin of the People's Republic of China. 天津天宝服装进出口有限公司 TIANJIN TIANBAO GARMENT I/E CO., LTD. TIANJIN, CHINA JUNE 7, 2011 --- Place and date, signature and stamp of certifying authority	It is hereby certified that the declaration by the exporter is correct. (CHINA COUNCIL FOR THE PROMOTION OF INTERNATIONAL TRADE) (TIANJIN) TIANJIN, CHINA JUNE 7, 2011 --- Place and date, signature and stamp of certifying authority

8. 出口货物报关

出口商将出口货物运抵海关监管区(如设立海关的港口、机场等)后,应于运输工具装货前24小时向海关申报出口货物。

对于法定检验检疫范围内的出口商品,出口商应当在报关前向出入境检验检疫机构报检,然后海关凭检验检疫机构签发的检验单证(如出境货物通关单)接受报关。

另外,在报关前,出口商还应先向海关进行"出口收汇核销单"的口岸备案,并如实向海关申报成交方式、成交单价、数量、总价、运费、保费等,同时将相关内容准确填写在核销单的相应栏目中。未进行口岸备案的核销单将不能用于出口报关。

一般出口货物的报关程序由四个环节构成,即出口申报、海关查验、缴纳税费、装运货物。

出口商持"出口货物报关单"和已完成口岸备案的"出口收汇核销单",随附"商业发票"、"装箱单",以及十联单的第五联"装货单"、第六联"场站收据副本"和第七联"场站收据"向海关申报货物出口。若为法定检验的货物,还需提交"出境货物通关单"。

经海关查验无误,并缴纳关税等税费后,海关在十联单的第五联"装货单"上加盖"海关放行章",并将该联及第六联、第七联退还出口商。

随着中国电子口岸的建设和发展,目前大部分口岸都采用了先提交电子数据申报,后提交纸质报关单的申报方式,也有部分口岸开始试行"无纸通关事后不交单"的业务模式。

在运载出口货物的运输工具结关离境后,海关还将按报关单位的申请,着手签发出口货物报关单的有关证明联,最常见的是"收汇核销联"和"出口退税专用单",并在"出口收汇核销单"上加盖"海关验讫章"。出口商通常要在完成出口通关后再等待一段时间,才能取得这些单证。

(1) 2011年6月8日,货物运抵港区后,场站人员根据"集装箱装箱单"(Container Load Plan,简称CLP)核对实际装箱情况,随后在CLP上签收、标注货物的进场日期,并将CLP装箱人/发货人联返还给天宝公司。

2011年6月9日,天宝公司向天津海关申报货物出口。填制出口货物报关单(第56页)、出口收汇核销单(第57页),并随附出境货物通关单(第49页)、商业发票(第41页)、装箱单(第40页)、十联单中的第五联装货单第六联和第七联,一并交给天津海关。

(2) 2011年6月10日,天宝公司收到天津海关加盖放行章的第五联"装货单"(第58页),及退回的第六联场站收据副本大副联(第43页)、第七联场站收据(第44页)。

中华人民共和国海关出口货物报关单

预录入编号：492850359 海关编号：2200201106097937560

出口口岸 天津海关	备案号		出口日期	申报日期 2011-06-09
经营单位 天津天宝服装进出口有限公司	运输方式 江海运输	运输工具名称 COSCO HELLAS		提运单号 COSU89302173
发货单位 天津天宝服装进出口有限公司	贸易方式 一般贸易	征免性质 一般征税		结汇方式 信用证
许可证号	运抵国（地区） 日本	指运港 神户		境内货源地 宝坻
批准文号 048932173	成交方式 CIF	运费 总价3000美元	保费 总价190.63美元	杂费
合同协议号 TE11PT005	件数 318	包装种类 纸箱	毛重（公斤） 3155	净重（公斤） 2160.360
集装箱号 CBHU75989732/20/2200 CBHU75989733/20/2200	随附单据 出境货物通关单：120500211005138000			生产厂家
标记唛码及备注 538A TJP2011-04-26 KOBE CARTON NO.1-219 MADE IN CHINA	538B TJP2011-04-26 KOBE CARTON NO.1-99 MADE IN CHINA			

项号	商品编号	商品名称、规格型号	数量及单位	最终目的国（地区）	单价	总价	币制	征免
01	6207910092	男式睡衣 MEN'S PAJAMAS	26850 件 2160.360 千克	日本	4.6290	124290.00	USD	照章征税

税费征收情况

录入员	录入单位	兹声明以上申报无讹并承担法律责任	海关审单批注及放行日期（签章）	
			审单	审价
报关员 3195460018314973 报关员 沈仲良 单位地址 天津市和平区岳阳道66号 邮编 300140 电话 022-58818844		申报单位（签章） 填报日期 2011-06-09	征税 查验	统计 放行

出口收汇核销单

存根

编号：04893173

出口单位：天津天宝服装进出口有限公司

单位代码：16796373-2

出口币种总价：US$124,290.00

收汇方式：信用证

预计收款日期：2011年7月5日

报关日期：2011年6月9日

备注：

此单报关有效期截止到 **2011年6月12日**

出口收汇核销单

编号：04893173

出口单位：天津天宝服装进出口有限公司

单位代码：16796373-2

类别	币种金额	日期	盖章
银行签注栏			

海关签注栏：

外汇局签注栏：

出口收汇核销专用联

编号：04893173

出口单位：天津天宝服装进出口有限公司

单位代码：16796373-2

货物名称	数量	币种总额
男式睡衣	26850件	US$124,290.00

报关单编号：220020110609797560

外汇局签注栏：

年　　月　　日（盖章）

未经核销此联不得撕开

Shipper (发货人)	D/R NO.(编号)	
TIANJIN TIANBAO GARMENT I/E CO., LTD. NO.66 YUEYANG ROAD, HEPING DISTRICT TIANJIN 300140, CHINA	COSU89302173	

装 货 单

第五联

场站收据副本

Consignee (收货人)	
TO ORDER	

Notify Party (通知人)	Received by the Carrier the Total number of containers or other packages or units stated below to be transported subject to the terms and conditions of the Carrier's regular form of Bill of Lading (for Combined Transport or port to port shipment) which shall be deemed to be incorporated herein. Date(日期): May 28, 2011
KANEYOSHI CO., LTD. 14-22 KYOMACHI-BORI 2-CHOME NISHI-KU, KOBE, JAPAN TEL: 06-6441-3325	

Pre-carriage by(前程运输)	Place of Receipt(收货地点)	
Vessel（船名）Voy. No.（航次） COSCO HELLAS / 013W	Port of loading（装货港） XINGANG	

场站章

Port of Discharge(卸货港) KOBE	Place of delivery(交货地点)	Final Destination for the Merchant's Reference (目的地)

Container No. (集装箱号)	Seal No.(封志号) Marks & Nos. (标志与号码)	No. of containers or pkgs (箱数或件数)	Kind of Packages: Description of Goods (包装种类与货名)	Gross Weight 毛重 (公斤)	Measurement 尺码 (立方米)
	538A TJP2011-04-26 KOBE CARTON NO.1-219 MADE IN CHINA	318CNTS	MEN'S PAJAMAS	3155.000KGS	49.646CBM
	538B TJP2011-04-26 KOBE CARTON NO.1-99 MADE IN CHINA		FREIGHT PREPAID		

TOTAL NUMBER OF CONTAINERS OR PACKAGES (IN WORDS) SAY THREE HUNDRED AND EIGHTEEN CARTONS ONLY
集装箱数或件数合计(大写)

Container No(箱号)	Seal No.(封志号)	Pkgs.(件数)	Container No(箱号)	Seal No.(封志号)	Pkgs.(件数)
			Received(实收)	By Terminal Clerk(场站员签字)	

FREIGHT & CHARGES	Prepaid at (预付地点)	Payable at (到付地点)	Place of Issue (签发地点) TIANJIN
	Total Prepaid (预付总额)	No. of Original B(s)/L (正本提单份数) THREE	Booking (订舱确认) APPROVED BY

Service Type on Receiving ☑ CY ☐ CFS ☐ DOOR	Service Type on Delivery ☑ CY ☐ CFS ☐ DOOR	签单章 (18)	°F °C
TYPE OF GOODS (种类) ☑ Ordinary (普通) ☐ Reefer (冷藏) ☐ Dangerous (危险品) ☐ Auto (裸装车辆) ☐ Liquid (液体) ☐ Live Animal (活动物) ☐ Bulk (散装)		危险品	Class: Property: IMDG Code Page: UN No.

9. 出口货物装运

出口货物装运流程如下：

● 出口商将加盖"海关放行章"的第五联，以及海关退还的第六联、第七联提交给堆场。堆场人员在货物进场、验收无误后，在第七联上签收并退还给出口商。

● 货物装船。

● 出口商向进口商发出装运通知。

● 出口商凭经场站签收的第七联"场站收据"向船公司换取正本提单。

在出口交易中，无论采用 FOB、CFR 还是 CIF 条件成交，在货物装船后，出口商均有义务及时向进口商发出装船通知。其目的除了通知进口商货物已经发运以便其做好接货准备外，在 FOB 和 CFR 条件下，该通知往往还是进口商办理货物运输投保的依据，因此，在这种条件下的装运通知也被称为投保通知。

(1) 2011 年 6 月 11 日，天宝公司将十联单中的五、六、七联（第 58、43、44 页）提交给堆场，堆场审核无误后，在第七联上签章并退回。

2011 年 6 月 12 日，货物顺利装船。

2011 年 6 月 12 日，向 Kaneyoshi Co., Ltd. 公司传真发出装运通知（第 60 页）。

(2) 2011 年 6 月 13 日，天宝公司凭第七联"场站收据"向船公司换取正本提单（第 61 页）。

天津天宝服装进出口有限公司
Tianjin Tianbao Garment I/E Co., Ltd.

FAX

To:	Kaneyoshi Co., Ltd.	**From:**	Tianjin Tianbao Garment I/E Co., Ltd.
Tel.No.:	06-6441-3325	**Tel. No.:**	+(86) 22 58818844
Page:	Page 1, Total 1 Page	**Date:**	June 12, 2011
Fax-No.:	06-6445-2391	**Fax-No.:**	+(86)22 58818766

SHIPPING ADVICE

CREDIT NUMBER: 866-10-014759

We hereby inform you that the goods under the above credit have been shipped on June 12, 2011. The details of shipment are stated below:

Date of Departure: June 12, 2011
Shipping Marks:
    538A   538B
    TJP2011-04-26   TJP2011-04-26
    KOBE   KOBE
    CARTON NO.1-219   CARTON NO.1-99
    MADE IN CHINA   MADE IN CHINA

Number of L/C: 866-10-014759
Number of B/L: COSU89302173
Number of Contract: TE11PT005
Number of Order: KANT-11-0426
Number of Cartons: 318 Cartons
Total Gross Weight: 3155 Kgs
Goods Value: USD124,290.00 CIF
Commodity: Men's Pajamas
Ocean Vessel: Cosco Hellas/013W
From: Xingang
To: Kobe
ETA: June 15, 2011

Yours sincerely,
Tianjin Tianbao Garment I/E Co., Ltd.

Deng Xin

中国天津和平区岳阳道 66 号
No.66 Yueyang Road, Heping District, Tianjin 300140, China
电话/Tel:86-22-58818844   传真/Fax:86-22-58818766   网址/Web: www.Tianbao.com.cn

中远集装箱运输有限公司
COSCO CONTAINER LINES

ORIGINAL
TLX:33057 COSCO CN
FAX:+86(021)65458984
PORT TO PORT OR COMBINED TRANSPORT BILL OF LADING

1. Shipper Insert Name Address and Phone / Fax	Booking No. 89302173	Bill of Lading No. COSU89302173
TIANJIN TIANBAO GARMENT I/E CO., LTD. NO.66 YUEYANG ROAD, HEPING DISTRICT TIANJIN 300140, CHINA	Export References	
2. Consignee Insert Name Address and Phone / fax TO ORDER	Forwarding agent and References	
	Point and Country of Origin	
3. Notify Party Insert Name Address and Phone /Fax (It is agreed that no responsibility shall attach to the Carrier or his agents for failure to notify) KANEYOSHI CO., LTD. 14-22 KYOMACHI-BORI 2-CHOME NISHI-KU, OSAKA, JAPAN TEL:06-6441-3325 FAX:06-6445-2391	Also Notify Party-routing & Instructions	
4. Combined Transport* Pre-Carriage by	5. Combined Transport* Place of Receipt		
6. Ocean Vessel Voy. No. COSCO HELLAS / 013W	7. Port of Loading TIANJIN XINGANG	Service Contract No.	Commodity Code
8. Port of Discharge KOBE	9. Combined Transport* Place of Delivery	Type of Movement FCL/FCL	

Marks & Nos. Container/Seal No.	No. of Container or Packages	Description of Goods (If Dangerous Goods, See Clause 20)	Gross Weight	Measurement
538A TJP2011-04-26 KOBE CARTON NO.1-219 MADE IN CHINA	318CTNS	MEN'S PAJAMAS SHIPPER'S LOAD, COUNT AND SEAL	3155.000KGS	49..646CBM
538B TJP2011-04-26 KOBE CARTON NO.1-99 MADE IN CHINA		**FREIGHT PREPAID**		
	CBHU75989732 /35737 /219CTNS /CY/CY /20'GP CBHU75989733 /35738 /99CTNS /CY/CY /20'GP			

Declared Cargo Value US$	Description of Contents for Shipper's Use Only (Not part of This B/L Contract)
10. Total Number of Containers and /or Packages (in words) Subject to Clause 7 Limitation	**SAY TWO TWENTY FEET CONTAINERS ONLY**

11. Freight & Charges	Revenue Tons	Rate	Per	Amount	Prepaid	Collect	Freight & Charges payable at/by

Received in external apparent good order and condition except otherwise noted. The total number of the packages or units stuffed in the container, the description of the goods and the weights shown in this Bill of Lading are furnished by the merchants, and which the carrier has no reasonable means of checking and is not a part of this Bill of Lading contract. The carrier has issued __3__ original Bill of Lading all of this tenor and date. one of the original Bill of Lading must be surrendered and endorsed or signed against the delivery of the shipment and whereupon any other original Bills of Lading shall be void. The merchants agree to be bound by the terms and conditions of this Bill of Lading as if ezch had personally signed this Bill of Lading.
*Applicable Only When Document Used as   a Combined Transport Bill of Lading.

Date Laden on Board   12 JUNE 2011
Signed by 天津中远集装箱船务代理有限公司
COSCO TIANJIN CONTAINER SHIPPING AGENCY CO., LTD
July. Smith
AS AGENT
For the Carrier. COSCO Container Lines

1106   Date of Issue   **12 JUNE 2011**   Place of Issue   **TIANJIN**   Signed for the Carrier: COSCO CONTAINER LINES

10. 出口交单结汇

随着国际贸易术语在国际货物买卖中的普遍采用以及银行的介入，"象征性交货"成为主要的国际贸易交易方式。"象征性交货"以单据买卖为核心，卖方以提交规定的单据作为其履行交货义务的象征和收取货款的依据，而买方则需凭合格的单据履行其付款的义务。

结汇单据的作用和地位在国际贸易中日益重要。特别在信用证结算方式下，银行独立于进口方和买卖合同，对受益人（出口商）承担付款责任，本着"单单一致，单证一致"的原则付款。

出口商在向银行交单议付前必须依据信用证、信用证修改书、《跟单信用证统一惯例》（UCP600）以及出口货物明细（或出口制单明细），对所有的议付单据进行细致严格的审核，本着严格相符的原则，将单据中所有的不符点消灭在交单之前，从而保证信用证项下的安全收汇。

作为出口货物的详尽说明，商业发票和装箱单在国内履约环节中曾多次被作为随附单据使用，但出口商在将其作为信用证项下的议付单据提交时，还是需要再次对其加以严格审核。

(1) 2011年6月13日，天宝公司将一套装运单据的副本（含商业发票、装箱单、提单、保险单）和一份原产地证明（第54页）传真给Kaneyoshi Co., Ltd.公司。

(2) 2011年6月14日，根据信用证及信用证修改书，天宝公司缮制并审核所有结汇单据。

2011年6月15日，在完成对全套结汇单据的复核和修改后，天宝公司向中国银行天津分行交单。

提交的文件和单据包括：

① 交单委托书（第64页）；

② 汇票，两联（第65页）；

③ 商业发票，一式三份，在原来办理国内手续发票基础上，严格按信用证要求重新缮制（第66页）；

④ 装箱单，一式三份，在原来办理国内手续装箱单基础上，严格按信用证要求重新缮制（第67页）；

⑤ 海运提单，正本一式三份（第60页），按信用证要求加注背书（第63页）；

⑥ 保险单，正本一式三份（第53页），按信用证要求加注背书（第63页）；

⑦ 品质检验证书，正本一式两份（第50页）；

⑧ 原产地证，正本一份（第54页）；

⑨ 寄单证明一份，见下图。

提单、保险单背书式样：

天津天宝服装进出口有限公司
TIANJIN TIANBAO GARMENT I/E CO., LTD.

_____
(SIGNATURE)

天津天宝服装进出口有限公司

Tianjin Tianbao Garment I/E Co., Ltd.

CERTIFICATE

CREDIT NUMBER: 866-10-014759

WE HEREBY STATING THAT SHIPPING DOCUMENTS INCLUDING INVOICE, PACKING LIST, B/L COPY HAVE BEEN SENT BY FAX TO APPLICANT(FAX 06-6445-2391) AFTER SHIPMENT.

天津天宝服装进出口有限公司
TIANJIN TIANBAO GARMENT I/E CO., LTD.

_____
(SIGNATURE)

出口信用证交单委托书

致： 中国银行 ___天津市___ 分行

兹随附下列银行正本信用证（修改书）及所属出口单据，请贵行根据国际商会跟单信用证统一惯例（UCP600）予以审核并办理寄单索汇：

开证行： THE MINATO BANK LTD. KOBE JAPAN	信用证号： 866-10-014759
	通知编号： BP70221563
发票号码： 01TE11PT005	发票金额： USD124,290.00

单据名称	汇票	发票	提单	副本提单	保险单/投保通知	装箱单	重量单	原产地证明	普惠制原产地证明	商检证书	受益人证明	船公司证明	装船通知副本	装船通知	寄单证明
份数	2	3	3		3	3		1		2					1

注：框内填写"√"是选择

付款指示：　　　　　　　　　　　核销单编号： 048932173

请将收汇款以　□ 原币或者，　√ 人民币划入我公司下列账户：

开户行： 中国银行天津分行　　　　账号： 086159-66795216843573

特别指示：
1. 邮寄方式　√ 快邮　　□ 普邮　　□ 指定快邮_____
2. 本次提交的正本信用证含 ___1___ 份正本修改书。

公司联系人姓名：　邓鑫　　　　公司签章

电话：58818844　传真：63753529　　　2011 年 6 月 15 日

以下栏目由我行填写

银行签收人：	签收日期：
改单/退单记录：	

注：本委托书一式3份，一份于交单时银行签收后退回本公司，一份结汇时作回单退公司，一份交由银行留底。

BILL OF EXCHANGE

No. __TE11PT-0616__

For __USD124, 290.00__   __TIANJIN   JUN.15, 2011__

   (amount in figure)   (place and date of issue)

At __*******SIGHT********__ of this   **FIRST**   Bill of Exchange (**SECOND** being unpaid) pay to____BANK OF CHINA, TIANJIN BRANCH_____ or order the sum of __SAY U.S. DOLLARS ONE HUNDRED AND TWENTY FOUR THOUSAND TWO HUNDRED AND NINETY ONLY__

                            （amount in words）

Drawn under   __THE MINATO BANK LTD., KOBE, JAPAN__

L/C No.   __866-10-014759__   dated   __MAY 4, 2011__

To: THE MINATO BANK LTD.   For and on behalf of
      14-22 KYOMACHI-BORI 2-CHOME   TIANJIN TIANBAO GARMENT I/E CO., LTD.
      NISHI-KU, KOBE, JAPAN

                                             (Signature)

BILL OF EXCHANGE

No. __TE11PT-0616__

For __USD124, 290.00__   __TIANJIN   JUN.15, 2011__

   (amount in figure)   (place and date of issue)

At __*******SIGHT********__ of this   **SECOND**   Bill of Exchange (**FIRST** being unpaid) pay to____BANK OF CHINA, TIANJIN BRANCH_____ or order the sum of __SAY U.S. DOLLARS ONE HUNDRED AND TWENTY FOUR THOUSAND TWO HUNDRED AND NINETY ONLY__

                            （amount in words）

Drawn under   __THE MINATO BANK LTD., KOBE, JAPAN__

L/C No.   __866-10-014759__   dated   __MAY 4, 2011__

To: THE MINATO BANK LTD.   For and on behalf of
      14-22 KYOMACHI-BORI 2-CHOME   TIANJIN TIANBAO GARMENT I/E CO., LTD.
      NISHI-KU, KOBE, JAPAN

                                             (Signature)

Tianjin Tianbao Garment I/E Co., Ltd.
No.66 Yueyang Road, Heping District
Tianjin 300140, China
Tel: 86-22-58818844
Fax:86-22-58818766

COMMERCIAL INVOICE

TO: KANEYOSHI CO., LTD.
    14-22 KYOMACHI-BORI 2-CHOME
    NISHI-KU, KOBE, JAPAN

INV.NO.: <u>01TE11PT005</u>
INV. DATE: <u>MAY 25, 2011</u>
S/C NO.: <u>TE11PT005</u>

FROM: <u>TIANJIN XINGANG</u>   TO: <u>KOBE</u>   SHIPPED BY <u>COSCO HELLAS / 013W</u>

MARKS & NOS.	DESCRIPTION OF GOODS		QUANTITY	UNIT PRICE	AMOUNT
538A TJP2011-04-26 KOBE CARTON NO. 1-219 MADE IN CHINA	MEN'S PAJAMAS (100% COTTON) 538A MEN'S PAJAMA TROUSERS 538B MEN'S NIGHT SHIRTS		 21900PCS 4950PCS	CIF KOBE USD4.50 USD5.20	 USD98,550.00 <u>USD25,740.00</u> USD124,290.00

538B
TJP2011-04-26
KOBE
CARTON NO.1-99
MADE IN CHINA

TERMS OF DELIVERY: CIF KOBE (INCOTERMS® 2010)
CREDIT NUMBER: 866-10-014759

TOTAL AMOUNT IN WORDS: SAY U.S. DOLLARS ONE HUNDRED AND TWENTY FOUR THOUSAND TWO HUNDRED AND NINETY ONLY.
TOTAL G.W./TOTAL N.W.:   3155.000KGS/2160.360KGS
TOTAL PACKAGES: 318CTNS

天津天宝服装进出口有限公司
TIANJIN TIANBAO GARMENT I/E CO., LTD.

_____
(SIGNATURE)

Tianjin Tianbao Garment I/E Co., Ltd.
No.66 Yueyang Road, Heping District,
Tianjin 300140, China
Tel: 86-22-58818844
Fax:86-22-58818766

PACKING LIST

TO: KANEYOSHI CO., LTD.　　　　　　　　　　　INV.NO.: 01TE11PT005
　　14-22 KYOMACHI-BORI 2-CHOME
　　NISHI-KU, KOBE, JAPAN　　　　　　　　　　INV. DATE: MAY 25, 2011

FROM: TIANJIN XINGANG　　TO: KOBE　　SHIPPED BY COSCO HELLAS / 013W

C/ NOS.	DESCRIPTION OF GOODS	PKG	QTY	G.W.	N.W.	MEAS
	MEN'S PAJAMAS (100% COTTON))					
538A TJP2011-04-26 KOBE CARTON NO.1-219 MADE IN CHINA	538A	219CTNS	21900PCS	2103.000KGS	1445.000KGS	33.646M³
538B TJP2011-04-26 KOBE CARTON NO.1-99 MADE IN CHINA	538B	99CTNS	4950PCS	1052.000KGS	715.360KGS	16.000 M³
	TOTAL:	318CTNS	26850 PCS	3155.000KGS	2160.360KGS	49.646M³

TOTAL PACKAGES IN WORDS: SAY THREE HUNDRED AND EIGHTEEN CARTONS ONLY

GROSS WEIGHT AND MEASUREMENTS PER EXPORT CARTON:
538A　GROSS WEIGHT: 9.60KGS.　MEASUREMENTS: 0.1536M³ (55×60×45CM)
538B　GROSS WEIGHT: 10.63KGS. MEASUREMENTS: 0.1616M3(55×60×49CM)

MARKS & NOS.: AS SHOWN IN C/NO.

TERMS OF DELIVERY: CIF KOBE (INCOTERMS® 2010)
CREDIT NUMBER:　866-10-014759

　　　　　　　　　　天津天宝服装进出口有限公司
　　　　　　　　　　TIANJIN TIANBAO GARMENT I/E CO., LTD.

　　　　　　　　　　_____
　　　　　　　　　　(SIGNATURE)

(CONTINUED TO NEXT PAGE)

11. 出口业务善后

当出口商向开证行(通过议付行)提交整套结汇单据后，业务就进入了善后阶段。

如果开证行对单据没有提出异议，在即期信用证项下得到付款，在远期信用证项下得到付款承诺。进口方在目的港接收货物后，本笔交易就可视为顺利完成。出口商要进行的善后工作包括：①拟写业务善后函；②办理收汇核销手续；③办理出口退税手续。

如果开证行认为单证不一致，就可能会拒付。这对于出口商来说就意味着以银行信用为基础的信用证付款方式的失效。收到银行的拒付通知后，出口商一定要先确定遭到拒付的原因，与国内议付行、交单行配合，做好应变工作，共同把因无法正常收汇而产生的风险和损失降至最低。同时还应迅速与进口方联系，寻求解决办法，尽量说服进口方付款并接受货物。

(1) 2011年6月29日，天宝公司收到天津海关加盖验讫章的出口货物报关单收汇核销联(第69页)、出口货物报关单出口退税专用(第70页)、出口收汇核销单(第71页)。

2011年6月30日，天宝公司收到中国银行天津分行开具的涉外收入申报单(即银行水单)(第72页)，获知开证行 The Minato Bank Ltd. 已付款，此笔交易顺利结汇。

(2) 2011年7月1日，天宝公司向 Kaneyoshi Co., Ltd. 公司去函，圆满结束本笔交易(第73页)。

(3) 2011年7月9日，天宝公司向外汇管理局办理出口收汇核销手续，提交涉外收入申报单(第72页)、出口货物报关单收汇核销联(第69页)和出口收汇核销单(第74页)。

(4) 2011年7月12日，天宝公司向国税局办理出口退税手续，提交增值税发票抵扣联(第74页)、商业发票(第66页)和出口货物报关单(出口退税专用)(第70页)、国家外汇管理局已加盖核销章的出口收汇核销单(出口退税专用)(第71页)。

中华人民共和国海关出口货物报关单

收汇核销联

预录入编号：492850359　　　　　　海关编号：2200201106097937560

出口口岸 天津海关	备案号	出口日期 2011-06-12	申报日期 2011-06-09
经营单位 天津天宝服装进出口有限公司	运输方式 江海运输	运输工具名称 COSCO HELLAS/ 013W	提运单号 COSU89302173
发货单位 天津天宝服装进出口有限公司	贸易方式 一般贸易	征免性质 一般征税	结汇方式 信用证
许可证号	运抵国（地区） 日本	指运港 神户	境内货源地 宝坻
批准文号 048932173	成交方式 CIF	运费 总价3000 美元	保费 总价190.63 美元	杂费
合同协议号 TE11PT005	件数 318	包装种类 纸箱	毛重（公斤） 3155	净重（公斤） 2160.360
集装箱号 CBHU75989732/20/2200 CBHU75989733/20/2200	随附单据 出境货物通关单：120500211005138000		生产厂家

标记唛码及备注
538A　　　　　　　　　　538B
TJP2011-04-26　　　　　　TJP2011-04-26
KOBE　　　　　　　　　　KOBE
CARTON NO.1-219　　　　CARTON NO.1-99
MADE IN CHINA　　　　　MADE IN CHINA

项号	商品编号	商品名称、规格型号	数量及单位	最终目的国（地区）	单价	总价	币制	征免
01	6207910092	男式睡衣 MEN'S PAJAMAS	26850 件 2160.360 千克	日本	4.6290	124290.00	USD	照章征税

税费征收情况

录入员　　录入单位	兹声明以上申报无讹并承担法律责任	海关审单批注及放行日期（签章）
		审单　　　审价
报关员 3195460018314973 报关员 沈仲良		
单位地址 天津市和平区岳阳道66号	申报单位（签章）	征税　　　统计
邮编 300140　电话 022-58818844	填报日期 2011-06-09	查验　　　放行

中华人民共和国海关出口货物报关单

出口退税专用

预录入编号：492850359　　　　海关编号：2200201106097937560

出口口岸 天津海关	备案号	出口日期 2011-06-12	申报日期 2011-06-09
经营单位 天津天宝服装进出口有限公司	运输方式 江海运输	运输工具名称 COSCO HELLAS/ 013W	提运单号 COSU89302173
发货单位 天津天宝服装进出口有限公司	贸易方式 一般贸易	征免性质 一般征税	结汇方式 信用证
许可证号	运抵国（地区） 日本	指运港 神户	境内货源地 宝坻
批准文号 048932173	成交方式 CIF	运费 总价 3000 美元	保费 总价 190.63 美元	杂费
合同协议号 TE11PT005	件数 318	包装种类 纸箱	毛重（公斤） 3155	净重（公斤） 2160.360
集装箱号 CBHU75989732/20/2200 CBHU75989733/20/2200	随附单据 出境货物通关单：120500211005138000		生产厂家

标记唛码及备注
538A　　　　　　　　538B
TJP2011-04-26　　　TJP2011-04-26
KOBE　　　　　　　　KOBE
CARTON NO.1-219　　CARTON NO.1-99
MADE IN CHINA　　　MADE IN CHINA

项号	商品编号	商品名称、规格型号	数量及单位	最终目的国（地区）	单价	总价	币制	征免
01	6207910092	男式睡衣 MEN'S PAJAMAS	26850 件 2160.360 千克	日本	4.6290	124290.00	USD	照章征税

税费征收情况

录入员	录入单位	兹声明以上申报无讹并承担法律责任	海关审单批注及放行日期（签章）
报关员 3195460018314973 报关员　沈仲良 单位地址 天津市和平区岳阳道66号 邮编 300140	电话 022-58818844	申报单位（签章） 填报日期 2011-06-09	审单　　　审价 征税　　　统计 查验　　　放行

出口收汇核销单（存根）

编号：048932173

出口单位：	天津天宝服装进出口有限公司		
单位代码：	16796373-2		
出口币种总价：	US$124,290.00		
收汇方式：	信用证		
预计收款日期：	2011年7月5日		
报关日期：	2011年6月9日		
备注：	此单报关有效期截止到 2011年6月12日		

出口收汇核销单（出口退税专用）

编号：048932173

出口单位：	天津天宝服装进出口有限公司		
单位代码：	16796373-2		
类别	币种金额	日期	盖章
银行签注栏			
海关签注栏：			
外汇签注栏：			

出口收汇核销单（海关留存联）

编号：048932173

出口单位：	天津天宝服装进出口有限公司		
单位代码：	16796373-2		
货物名称	数量	币种总额	
男式睡衣	26850 件	US$124,290.00	
报关单编号：	22002011060979375 60		
外汇局签注栏：	年　月　日（盖章）		

未经核销此联不得撕开

出口收汇核销专用联	涉外收入申报单（对公）		日期： 2011-6-29
			时间： 16:35:12
			页数： 1

根据《国际收支统计申报办法》（1995年8月30日由国务院批准），特制发本申报单。　　制表机关：国家外汇管理局
国家外汇管理局和有关银行为您的申报内容保密

出口收汇核销专用联

申报号码：120107 0001 31 110609 N001		申报日期：2011-06-30	
申报银行：120107000222 中国银行天津分行国际业务部（营业）		企业注册所在地：120107	
收款人编码： 761256738　分公司代号 000　收款人名称：天津天宝服装进出口有限公司			
人民币账号：		外汇账号： 086159-66795216843573	
结算方式： 信用证		付款人名称：THE MINATO BANK LTD., KOBE, JAPAN	
收入款金额： USD 美元		其中　结汇金额：	0
USD124,290.00		现汇金额：	124,103.56
收款日期： 2011-06-29　是否已收入收款账户：是		其他金额	0
银行业务编号：BP70221563			

扣费信息　出口收汇核销项下扣费明细					
项目	银行费用	回扣	佣金		保费
国内扣费	币种	USD			
	金额	186.44	0	0	0
国外扣费	币种	USD			
	金额	0	0	0	0
项目	还贷款	租赁款	退款	赔款	其他
国内扣费	币种				
	金额	0	0	0	0
国外扣费	币种				
	金额	0	0	0	0

以下内容请企业根据本笔交易如实填写

付款人国别、地区： JP 日本	发票或合同号码：01TE11PT005 / TE11PT005		
国际收支交易编码： 0101	交易附言：一般贸易男式睡衣		
报关单号码：22002011060979937560	填报人电话：022-58818844		
	报关日期	币种	报关金额
	2011-06-09	USD	124,290.00

收汇核销号码：	如果本笔收入款为退款，请填写该笔收入对应的原对外付款申报号码：	
核销号码	申报号码	完全退款
048932173		

银行柜员信息	银行操作人：卢敏华	操作日期：2011-06-029
	银行复核人：卢敏华	复核日期：2011-06-030
企业人员信息	填报人： 761256736	
	企业操作员：761256736	操作日期：2011-06-030
	企业复核人：761256736	复核日期：2011-06-030
外管局信息	审批编号：	
	查复性申报原因：	
	是否查复性申报： 否	

报表结束

天津天宝服装进出口有限公司
Tianjin Tianbao Garment I/E Co., Ltd

1-July-2011

Mr. Genichiro Sata
Kaneyoshi Co., Ltd.
14-22 Kyomachi-Bori 2-Chome
Nishi-Ku, Kobe, JAPAN

Dear Mr. Sata,

  We are glad to receive the proceeds under L/C No. 866-10-014759 against S/C No. TE11PT005.

  We appreciate your cooperation during the past months and are pleased to see the first transaction going through smoothly.

  We trust that the goods will arrive at Kobe safe and sound and give you complete satisfaction.

  We look forward to the pleasure of doing further business with you in the near future.

Yours sincerely,
Tianjin Tianbao Garment I/E Co., Ltd.

Deng Xin

中国天津和平区岳阳道 66 号
No.66 Yueyang Road, Heping District, Tianjin 300140, China
电话/Tel:86-22-58818844   传真/Fax:86-22-58818766   网址/Web: www.Tianbao.com.cn

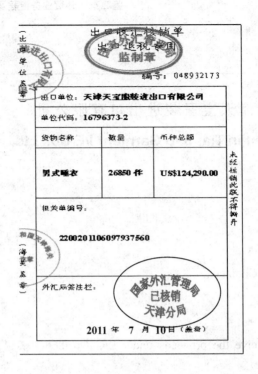

12. 进口商付款赎单

信用证方式下，开证行根据信用证条款审核单据后，履行付款义务，之后将单据交进口商复审，要求付款赎单。

开证行接到国外议付行寄来的单据，首先根据信用证规定的条款，全面、逐项地审核单证之间、单单之间是否相符，并根据国外议付行的寄单索偿通知书，核对单据的种类、份数以及汇票、发票与索偿通知书所列金额是否正确。银行对信用证未规定的单据将不予审核。银行审单的合理时间是不超过收到单据次日起的五个银行工作日。审核无误后，凭议付行的寄单索偿通知，填制进口单据发送清单，附上全部单据送开证申请人签收，经开证申请人全面审核无误后办理付款。银行将全部单据交给开证申请人，开证申请人可以凭以提货。

目前国内银行通常采用变通的审单做法，即开证行在接到国外寄来单据以后，通常是对寄单面函中的内容(如确认所附单据属于相关的信用证号码项下，单据中的金额与面函中提及的金额是否一致，是否提及有任何不符点，是否凭担保函或有保留的付款、承兑或议付等)进行重点审核，而对单据只是粗审，找出单据中较明显的不符点，批注在来单通知书上，连同单据交开证申请人，并请其告知开证行对不符点单据的处理意见，据此开证行决定是否对外拒付。

银行采用此方法有其合理之处：只有在申请人拒收时，开证行才对外拒付，由此开证行可以大大减少对外拒付的次数，从而维护良好的对外形象；可以简化手续，减少银行审单工作量；减少银行保存的单据份数；开证申请人比银行对货物规格等条款内容更为熟悉。

申请人接到单据(实质上是银行暂借单据给申请人)在办理对外付款之前，一定要对单据妥善保管，以便在单证不符拒付时可以对外退单。

2011 年 6 月 22 日，Kaneyoshi Co., Ltd. 收到开证行的付款赎单通知(第 76 页)。

The Minato Bank Ltd.
2-1-1, Sannomiya-cho, Chuo-ku,
Kobe, 651-0193 Japan

Tel:+ 06-6455-3465

June 22, 2011
KANEYOSHI CO., LTD.
14-22 KYOMACHI-BORI 2-CHOME
NISHI-KU, KOBE, JAPAN

Dear Sirs,
As instructed by your fax of June 14, we have just accepted for your account a bill for US$124,290.00 drawn by Tianjin Tianbao Garment I/E Co., Ltd. for the consignment of 318 cartons of Men's Pajamas to you by MV "COSCO HELLAS / 013W". We have debited your account with this amount and our charges amounting to US$124,474.00.

The vessel left Tianjin on June 12 and is due to arrive in Kobe on June 15. The shipping documents for the consignment are now with us and we shall be glad if you will arrange to collect them.

Yours faithfully
For MINATO BANK LTD.,.

Arina Tanemura
Arina Tanemura

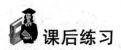 课后练习

Design a transaction according to the following Sales Confirmation and L/C. Write related letters and make related documents.

Shanghai Universal Trading Co.,Ltd.
Rm.1201-1216 Mayling Plaza,
131 Dongfang Rd.,
Shanghai, 200120, China P.O.Box 1783
Tel:86-21-58818844
Fax:86-21-58818876

SALES CONFIRMATION

S/C No.: 08HY-TIV0373
S/C Date: April 5, 2008

To: Tivolian Trading B.V.
P.O.Box 1783 Heiman Dullaertolein
3024CA Rotterdam, Netherlands

We hereby confirm having sold to you the following goods on terms and conditions as specified below:

Article No.	Name of Commodity & Specifications	Quantity	Unit Price	Amount
	Plush Toys details as per the samples dispatched by the seller on March 16, 2008			CIF Rotterdam
KB0278	Twin Bear	504 sets	US$9.60	US$4,838.40
KB5411	Twin Bear in Ballet Costume	504 sets	US$11.50	US$5,796.00
KB0677	Brown Bear with Red Bow	536 sets	US$14.50	US$7,772.00
KB7900	Bear in Pink T-shirt	536 sets	US$15.40	US$8,254.40
	Total:	2080 sets		US$26,660.80

Total Amount in Words: SAY U.S. DOLLARS TWENTY SIX THOUSAND SIX HUNDRED AND SIXTY AND CENTS EIGHTY ONLY.

Packing: KB0278 & KB5411: the label "CE/IMP.087" to be attached to each piece,
KB0677 & KB7900: the label "F-TOYS 228" to be attached to each piece,
KB0278 & KB5411 to be packed in cartons of 4 sets each, equally assorted in one 20'FCL,
KB0677 & KB7900 to be packed in cartons of 8 sets each, equally assorted in one 20'FCL,
Total 386 cartons in Two 20' FCL.
Shipment: To be effected during May 2008 from Shanghai, China to Rotterdam, Netherlands.
Insurance: To be covered by the seller for 110% of invoice value against all risks and war risk as per the Ocean Marine Cargo Clauses of PICC dated Jan.1, 1981.
Payment: The buyer should open through a bank acceptable to the seller an irrevocable letter of credit payable at sight for 100% of the contract value to reach the seller by the end of April 2008 and valid for negotiation in China until the 15th day after the date of shipment.

Confirmed by:

THE SELLER   **THE BUYER**
Shanghai Universal Trading Co., Ltd.

(signature)   (signature)

```
2008 APR 18    07:29:18                    LOGICAL TERMINAL 1345
MT S700    ISSUE OF A DOCUMENTARY CREDIT    PAGE 00001
                                            FUNC SWPR3
                                            UMR 20737727
MSGACK DWS7651 AUTH OK, KEY B6852DT5E5896841, BKCHCNBJ BKCHSGSG RECORD
BASIC HEADER           F    01   BKCHCNBJA300    2576      87612
APPLICATION HEADER     O    700   7992 080418 FVLBNL2RXXX6385 938271 080418 379 N
                                  F. VAN LANSCHOT BANKIERS N.V.
                                  *ROTTERDAM
                                  *NETHERLANDS
USER HEADER SERVICE CODE    103:
        BANK PRIORITY       113:
        MSG USER REF.       108:
        INFO. FROM CI       115:
SEQUENCE OF TOTAL          *27  :1/1
FORM OF DOC. CREDIT        *40A : IRREVOCABLE
APPLICABLE RULES            40E : UCP600
DOC. CREDIT NUMBER         *20  : AM/VA07721SLC
DATE OF ISSUE               31C : 080418
DATE AND PLACE OF EXPIRY   *31D : DATE 080609 PLACE NETHERLANDS
APPLICANT                  *50  : TIVOLIAN TRADING B.V.
                                  P.O.BOX 1783, HEIMAN DULLAERTOLEIN, 3024CA
                                  ROTTERDAM, NETHERLANDS
BENEFICIARY                *59  : SHANGHAI UNIVERSAL TRADING CO.,LTD.
                                  MAYING PLAZE, 131 DONGFANG ROAD,
                                  SHANGHAI 200120, CHINA
CURRENCY CODE, AMOUNT      *32B : CURRENCY USD AMOUNT 26660.80
AVAILABLE WITH/BY          *41D : ANY BANK BY NEGOTIATION
DRAFT AT…                   42C : AT 30DAYS AFTER SIGHT FOR FULL INVOICE VALUE
DRAWEE                      42A : F. VAN LANSCHOT BANKIERS N.V.
                                  ROTTERDAM, NETHERLANDS
PARTIAL SHIPMENTS           43P : ALLOWED
TRANSSHIPMENT               43T : PROHIBITED
LOADING ON BOARD/DISPATCH/TAKING IN CHARGE AT/FROM   44A : SHANGHAI
FOR TRANSPORT TO…           44B : ROTTERDAM
LATEST DATE OF SHIP.        44C :080525
DESCRIPT. OF GOODS AND/OR SERVICES           45A :
    4 ITEMS OF TOTAL 2088 SETS OF PLUSH TOYS AS PER APPLICANT'S ORDER
    NUMBER TIV-PO-CSH0873 AND BENEFICIARY'S CONTRACT NUMBER 08HY-TIV0373
    LABEL :CE/IMP.087 FOR ARTICLES KB0278, KB5411
    LABEL :F-TOYS 228 FOR ARTICLES KB0677, KB7900
    TERMS OF DELIVERY :CIF ROTTERDAM(INCOTERMS 2000)
    PACKING IN NEUTRAL SEAWORTHY EXPORT CARTONS SUITABLE FOR LONG DISTANCE OCEAN
    TRANSPORTATION
    SHIPPING MARKS:      CE/IMP.087
                         TIV-PO-CSH0873
                         ROTTERDAM
                         CARTON NO.1 AND UP
                         FOLLOWED BY: ARTICLE NUMBER AND
                         F-TOYS 228
                         TIV-PO-CSH0873
                         ROTTERDAM
                         CARTON NO.1 AND UP
                         FOLLOWED BY: ARTICLE NUMBER
    ALL OF THE ABOVE MUST BE STATED ON THE INVOICE AND PACKING LIST.
```

```
2008 APR 18    07:29:18                LOGICAL TERMINAL 1345
MT S700      ISSUE OF A DOCUMENTARY CREDIT      PAGE 00001
                                                FUNC SWPR3
                                                UMR 20737727
```

DOCUMENTS REQUIRED   46A :
  +SIGNED COMMERCIAL INVOICE IN QUINTUPICTE MADE OUT IN THE NAME OF
   APPLICANT INDICATING FOB VALUE AND THE ORIGIN OF THE GOODS SHIPPED.
  +PACKING LIST/WEIGHT MEMO IN TRIPLICATE MENTIONING TOTAL NUMBER OF CARTONS
   AND GROSS WEIGHT AND MEASUREMENTS PER EXPORT CARTON.
  +2/3 OF ORIGINAL CLEAN ON-BOARD MARINE BILL OF LADING, PLUS 3 N.N.-COPIES MADE OUT:" TO
   ORDER", AND BLANK ENDORSED MARKED:" FREIGHT PREPAID" SHOWING AS NOTIFY THE
   APPLICANT(GIVING FULL NAME, ADDRESS AND PHONE NUMBERS) AND INDICATING THE NAME AND ADDRESS
   OF THE CARRIER'S AGENT AT THE PORT OF DISCHARGE.
  +FULL SET 3/3 OF MARINE INSURANCE POLICY OR CERTIFICATE, ENDORSED IN BLANK FOR 120 PERCENT
   OF FULL CIF VALUE, COVERING INSTITUTE CARGO CLAUSES(A) AND INSTITUTE WAR CLAUSES-CARGO.
  +COPY OF G.S.P. CERTIFICATE OF ORIGIN FORM A IN DUPLICATE STATING THAT THE GOODS ARE OF
   CHINESE ORIGIN.
  +BENEFICIARY'S CERTIFICATE STATING THAT ONE SET OF NON-NEGOTIALBLE SHIPPING DOCUMENTS
   TOGETHER WITH THE 1/3 ORIGINAL B/L AND ORIGINAL GSP FORM A HAVE BEEN SENT TO THE APPLICANT
   BY DHL WITHIN 72 HOURS AFTER SHIPMENT.
  +ORIGINAL AND COPY OF QUALITY INSPECTION CERTIFICATE ISSUED AND SIGNED BY THE APPLICANT.
  +COPY OF BENEFICIARY'S FAX SENT TO APPLICANT (FAX-NO.:+(31)104767422) WITHIN
   2 WORKING DAYS AFTER SHIPMENT INDICATING DATE OF DEPARTURE, SHIPPING MARKS, NUMBERS OF
   LC, B/L, CONTRACT AND ORDER AS WELL AS NUMBER OF CARTONS
   TOGETHER WITH THE TOTAL GROSS WEIGHT AND GOODS VALUE.
CHARGES   71B : ALL BANKING CHARGES INCLUDING OPENING FEE ARE FOR
                                  BENEFICIALRY'S ACCOUNT.
PERIOD OF PRESENTATION   48 :DOCUMENTS TO BE PRESENTED WITHIN 15 DAYS AFTER THE DATE
                                 OF ISSUANCE OF TRANSPORT DOCUMENT(S) BUT WITHIN THE VALIDITY
                                 OF THIS CREDIT.
CONFIRMATION INSTRUCTIONS   *49 :WITHOUT
ADDITIONAL CONDITIONS   47A:
  +ALL DOCUMENTS MUST INDICATE THIS CREDIT NUMBER.
  +THE CARRYING VESSEL SHOULD BELONG TO CONFERENCE LINE AND NOT MORE THAN 20 YEARS OLD. A
   CERTIFICATE TO THIS EFFECT ISSUED BY THE SHIPPING COMPANY TO BE PRESENTED WITH THE L/C
   DOCUMENTS UPON NEGOTIATION.
  +ALL DOCUMENTS TO BE SENT TO F.VAN LANSCHOT BANKIERS N.V. WESTERSINGEL
   74 3015 LB ROTTERDAM TEL:+31(0)10 440 20 20 FAX +31(0) 10 440 20 90
       IN ONE LOT BY INTERNATIONAL COURIER SERVICE.
INSTRUCTION TO THE PAYING/ACCEPTING/NEGOTIATING BANK   78:
  +T.T. REIMBURSEMENT IS NOT ACCEPTABLE
  +A DISREPANCY FEE OF USD50.00 WILL BE DEDUCTED FROM THE PROCEEDS IF DOCUMENTS ARE PRESENTED
   WITH DISCREPANCY(IES)AND ACCEPTANCE OF SUCH DISCREPANT DOCUMENTS WILL NOT IN ANY WAY ALTER
   THE TERMS AND CONDITIONS OF THIS CREDIT.
  +UPON RECEIPT OF CORRECT DOCUMENTS BY US, WE SHALL COVER THE NEGOTIATING BANK AS PER THEIR
   INSTRUCTIONS, IN THE CURRENCY OF THIS CREDIT ONLY.
SENDER TO RECEIVER INFORMATION   72: /PHONBEN/
TRAILER   <MAC:9KE93827><CHK:975CIE072287>

第三单元　建立业务关系

第三章　建立业务关系与资信调查

一、业务背景知识

与客户建立业务关系是正式开展进出口业务的重要步骤，无论是买方还是卖方，要扩大业务，都要在巩固原有关系的基础上，不断寻找新的业务伙伴，不断建立新的业务关系。

1. 如何获取潜在客户信息

企业可以通过分析相关资料、经第三方介绍或网络搜寻的方法找到潜在客户。

（1）资料分析法

企业可以通过分析相关统计资料、名录类资料、报章类资料等来寻找潜在客户。

统计资料包括相关部门的统计调研报告、行业在报纸或期刊上刊登的统计调研资料、行业团体公布的调查统计资料等。

名录类资料包括国内外出版的企业名录、会员名录、协会名录、电话黄页、公司年鉴、企业年鉴等。

报章类资料包括报纸和杂志上的广告、产业或金融方面的信息、行业动向、同行活动情形等。

（2）经第三方介绍

企业通常可以通过下列第三方渠道获取潜在客户信息：现有的贸易伙伴；国内外银行；国内外的贸易促进机构或友好协会，如我国的贸促会；我国驻外使馆商务处或外国驻华使馆，一般来讲，我国驻外使馆对当地主要厂商的经营范围、能力和资信较为熟悉和了解；参加国内外展览会、交易会，这类活动的优点是能和客户直接见面，联系的范围广；利用国内外的专业咨询公司介绍客户，他们的业务关系中有许多具有一定影响力、专业经验和能力的客户。

（3）通过网络搜寻

通过网络寻找潜在客户主要可以通过以下网站：①大型的搜索引擎，如 Google，Baidu，Yahoo，Excite 等，一般用关键词搜索；②该行业的行业网，每个行业几乎都有行业网站，可用关键词搜索，一般会在这些网页上看到会员列表和相关链接；③通过大型的搜索引擎寻找目标国的黄页网站和工商企业目录；④大型的公司数据库，如美国的 THOMPSON 网等；⑤B2B 网站，很多 B2B 网上有生产商的信息；⑥名录网站；⑦大使馆经济参赞处的网站；⑧展会的网站；⑨工具网站，如 Alexa 工具网站，Alexa.com 是世界最著名的电子商务网站 amazon.com 公司的成员企业，是互联网上最权威的第三方流量监测网站。

2. 资信调查的渠道

当买卖双方建立业务关系，并有意达成首笔交易，尤其是涉及大笔资金的交易时，切实了解对方公司的信用、财务状况、履约情况是非常重要的。当然，这些情况也可以从对方提供的公司介绍中获得。但在公司介绍中一般总是强调自己的优势，因而有必要从第三方获取较为中立、客观的资料，但是其费用比较高。

第三方可以是与对方有业务联系的其他公司、银行、商会，我们称之为"证明人"。通常，对方会主动或应要求提供证明人，但是它当然会挑选为自己说好话的证明人。因此，对来自这些证明人的报告应当谨慎对待。相对来讲，银行的报告较为可靠，但银行通常不会透露其客户的情况，除非这类查询来自他的同业银行。因此，通过自己的往来银行获取对方银行提供的证明材料是最可靠、便捷的方法之一。

此外，通过我驻外机构和在实际业务活动中对客户进行考察所得的材料，一般比较具体可靠，对业务的开展有较大的参考价值。外国出版的企业名录、厂商年鉴以及其他有关资料，对了解客户的经营范围和活动情况也有一定的参考价值。

二、例信

1. Establishing Business Relations

(1) From the Seller to the Prospective Buyer

Dear Sirs,

We learn from the Peruvian Consulate here that you are a prospective buyers of Chinese Cotton Piece Goods. As this item falls within the scope of our business activities, we shall be pleased to enter into direct business relations with you at an early date.

To give you a general idea of the various kinds of cotton piece goods now available for export, we enclose a brochure and a price list. Quotations and sample books will be airmailed to you upon receipt of your specific inquiry.

For our business and financial standing, we may refer you to our bankers, Bank of China, Shanghai branch (address: ..., Tel: ...).

We look forward to your favorable reply.

Yours faithfully,

(2) From the Buyer to the Seller

Dear Sirs,

We got your address through your *www.cnart.com.cn*.

We are an importer from Asia and have excellent connections with major dealers here of light industrial products. Please send us some information concerning such items and also the prices.

At the same time, if you expose your products at any fair in China, please let us know the name and date of it so that we may visit you.

We look forward to hearing from you soon.

Kindest Regards,

2. Status Enquiries

Dear Sirs,

Credit Inquiry on the Maryland, Inc.
Towson 9, Maryland, U. S. A.

The subject company is now offering to represent us in the sale of our Sewing Machines, and has referred us to your Bank for detailed information about its credit standing, business capacity and character. We shall highly appreciate it if you will give us your frank opinion on these points regarding the company.

Any information you may give us will be treated strictly in confidence.

Thank you in advance.

Yours faithfully,

(Favorable reply)

Gentlemen:

The Maryland Inc.

The captioned company you inquired about by your letter of September 15th, 2008, has been maintaining an account with us for the past 20 years, during which they have never failed to meet their obligations. Their balance sheets of recent years enclosed will show you that their import business in Sewing Machines has been managed and operated under a satisfactory condition.

We believe that they owe their reputable position among the local wholesalers in our district to their steady and sincere way of conducting business.

Please note that this information is furnished without any responsibility on our part and should be held strictly confidential.

Yours truly,

(Unfavorable reply)

Dear Sirs,

<u>the Maryland Inc.</u>

The subject company you inquired about in your letter of June 25th, 2005, we are sorry to say, has been unsatisfactory.

The company still owes an amount of money for a purchase made a year ago. They can not duly clear off their balance outstanding.

May we ask you to treat this information as strictly confidential without responsibility on our bank.

Yours faithfully,

三、信件主要内容

1. 建立业务关系的信函

(1) 信息来源

作为贸易商，可以有各种途径来认识客户，如通过驻外使馆商务参赞处、商会、银行或第三方公司的介绍；或在企业名录、各种传媒广告、互联网上查得；或在交易会、展览会上认识。在建立业务关系时，发函者通常都会告知对方自己是通过何种途径得到对方信息的。

- We learned from the Commercial Counselor's Office of our Embassy in your country that you are in the market for Chinese handicraft.
- Mr. Jacques, Canadian Ambassador in Beijing, has recommended you to us as a leading importer in Korea of lightweight batteries for vehicles.
- We have obtained your name and address from the Internet.
- Our market survey showed that you are the largest importer of cases and bags.

(2) 致函目的

一般来说，建交函是以扩大交易地区及对象、建立长期业务关系为目的的。

- In order to expand the sales of our products into South America, we are writing to you to seek cooperation possibilities.
- We are writing to you to establish long-term trade relations with you.
- We wish to express our desire to enter into business relationship with you.

(3) 公司介绍

包括对公司性质、业务范围、宗旨等基本情况的概述，以及对公司某些竞争优势的凸显，如经验丰富、供货渠道稳定、有广泛的销售网等。必要时告知对方本公司的往来银行以便对方通过银行查询。

- We are a leading company with many years of experience in machinery export business.
- We enjoy a good reputation internationally in the circle of textile.

- We have our principle as "Clients' needs come first".
- Located in Shanghai, we take the advantage to set up our solidifying production basis in coastal and inland areas.
- For our credit standing, please refer to the following bank: ...

(4) 产品介绍

建立业务关系信函中的产品介绍,大致有两种形式:在较明确对方需求时,选取某种特定的产品进行具体推荐性介绍;否则,通常只就公司经营产品的整体情况,如质量标准、价格水平、目前销路等,做较为笼统的介绍。附上目录、报价单或另寄样品供对方参考也是公司经常采取的做法。

- Art No. 76 is our newly launched one with superb quality, fashionable design, and competitive price.
- We have a good variety of colours and sizes to meet your different needs.
- Our products are enjoying popularity in Asian markets.
- To give you a general idea of our products, we are enclosing our catalogue for your reference.

(5) 盼望答复

- Your comments on our products or any information on your market demand will be really appreciated.
- We are looking forward to your specific enquiries.

2. 资信调查的信函

(1) 说明写信意图

- Our prospective customer ABC Company has given us your name as banking references.
- They state that they have done business with you for the past two years and have given us the name of your company as a reference.

(2) 说明想要调查的细节

- Will you please inform us frankly whether you consider a credit to the extent of USD5,000,000 as a risk?
- We should appreciate it if you would provide us with reliable information respecting Messrs J. C. Maxell Company. We wish to know if their financial standing is considered strong.

(3) 保证保守秘密

- Any information we receive from you, of course, will be held in strict confidence.
- We thank you for your courtesy and assure you of strict confidence.

3. 回复资信调查的信函

(1) 针对询问客观评价

- We have completed our inquiry concerning the firm mentioned in your letter of August

15, 2005 and that we must advise you to consider their request with caution.
- We inform you that we can give nothing but favorable information about the firm in question.
- Their chief line is in the import and export of all kinds of foods, trading principally with China, Japan, Germany, Britain and America. Their supplier's business with them is reported to have been satisfactory. The bankers have a high regard for their operating ability and financial standing.

(2) 免责申明和保密要求
- The above information is strictly confidential and is given without any liability on our part.
- We would advise you to pay more cautious attention to any trade with them, however, it is our personal opinion, and we wish you to make further enquiries.

四、重点用语

1. 介绍业务范围

(1) fall within v. 属于……的范畴

① As the above-mentioned goods fall within the scope of our business activities, your letter has been passed on to us for attention.

(2) line n. 行业,行当

① We have been in the bakery line for 20 years.

② Textiles are our line.

(3) handle v. 做(某项买卖),买,卖

① We are a state-owned corporation, handling the export of canned goods.

② This shop handles meat and groceries(食品杂货).

(4) deal in v. 经营

① This shop deals in woolen goods.

② Most foreign trading companies in West Africa deal in rubber, cocoa and vegetable oils.

(5) dealer, exporter, importer, wholesaler, retailer

2. 建立业务关系

(1) To establish business relations with... 与……建立业务关系

(2) To enter into business relationship with... 与……建立业务关系

We have established close business relationship with more than a dozen of manufacturers.

3. 提供资信证明

(1) credit standing 资信状况

(2) financial standing 财务状况

refer to v. 引……去查询询问，查询

① Anyhow, our bank should look into your credit standing, and then make a decision.

② We refer you to The Bank of Switzerland if you wish to make any inquiries on our credit standing.

③ As to our credit standing, please refer to our correspondent bank, Bank of London.

 课后练习

1. Translate the following sentences into English.

（1）几个月前，我方有机会在上海世博会中看到贵方产品，对其品质与合理的价格印象极为深刻。

（2）收到贵公司 2008 年 12 月 3 日来函，我方非常高兴地知道贵公司有意和我方在纺织产品方面开展贸易合作。

（3）为使贵公司了解我公司的罐头食品，我方将通过航空邮件寄去最新的产品目录。在接到贵公司的具体询价后，我方将寄去报价和样品。

（4）我们的潜在客户 Messrs E. Sheen & Co. 将贵行指定为他们的资信证明人，希望贵行对该公司财务状况和可靠性提出你们的意见。

（5）虽然那家公司是一家历史悠久的公司，但是企业已经连续三年发生亏损。他们的债务已高达 1.5 亿美元，在过去的 3 年中他们总是拖延支付，在我们看来，企业的亏损是由于他们的不良管理造成的。

（6）根据我们的记录，该公司自在我行开户以来从未拖欠银行账单。我们每月给予他们的安全授信额度为 £ 3,000。此外，由于诚信待人、履约及时，他们在业界享有很好的信誉。

2. Translate the letter into English.

XX 先生，

　　我们是本市一流的糖果公司，同各大城市食品店有着广泛的联系。为了生产糖果糕点，我公司需要长期固定的核桃仁供应。截至目前，我公司一直从东南亚国家进口，但最近由于价格波动，供应已不可靠。为此，我公司愿与贵公司建立直接业务关系。

　　现请贵公司按竞争价格发来 3 吨二级核桃仁报价，9 月份交货，并请注明有关各项贸易条件。

　　关于我公司财务状况，请向我公司往来银行 Bank of London（地址：……）了解。希望能尽早同贵公司建立业务关系。

　　此致

敬礼

3. Begin a letter to a foreign firm by identifying yourself and then stating that you want a brochure on their fine chemicals. Conclude the letter with a request.

4. Write a brief but courteous letter sending the catalogue and price list requested by the receiver in previous letter.

第四单元　合同的达成

国际货物买卖合同的磋商一般可概括为四个环节：询盘、发盘、还盘和接受。其中发盘和接受是必经的环节，在法律上分别称为"要约"和"承诺"，具有特定的法律效力。经过有效的要约与承诺，合同成立。还盘可视为一项新的"要约"。

各国法律都规定，一项合同，除买卖双方就交易条件通过要约与承诺达成协议后，还需具备相应的法律要件才能生效，包括：当事人的签约能力、合同的对价、合同内容合法、合同形式符合法律规定、当事人的意思表示必须真实等。

本单元介绍国际货物买卖的要约邀请、要约与承诺函，以及具有一定形式的合同书。

第四章 要约邀请

一、业务背景知识

要约邀请是指交易一方向对方传达交易意向，希望对方向自己发出要约。要约邀请不是交易磋商的必经步骤，对于发出者和接收者均无法律上的约束力。询盘和报虚盘是国际贸易业务中常见的两种要约邀请。

询盘又称询价，是指买方为了购买或卖方为了销售而向对方提出有关交易条件的询问。其内容可以是询问价格，也可以是询问一项或几项交易条件。报虚盘是指交易一方提出了具体的交易条件，但又有所保留，表示不受约束。

二、例信

1. Enquiries and Replies

(1)

Dear Mr...

  We learn from your Embassy that you are manufacturing and exporting a variety of textile machines. As there is a demand here for high-quality knitting machines, we will appreciate your sending us a copy of your illustrated catalogue, with details of your prices and terms of payment. It would be most helpful if you could also supply information concerning the types of fabric to be processed and the type of yarn.

Sincerely yours,

(Reply)

Dear Mr...

  We thank you for your enquiry of 9th January and are pleased to tell you that we manufacture and export different types of textile machinery, in particular, knitting machines.

We can supply fabric setting machinery and printing equipment for cotton and polyester materials. We can also supply drying and calendaring machines to take care of the finishing to most of the knitted fabrics.

Would you please supply us with more information concerning the fabrics to be processed so that we may send you the quotation for the most suitable type of knitting machines we are able to supply.

We enclose some brochure to illustrate the type of machines we manufacture. We have already sold some of those machines to China and we are now represented there by the Engineering Export Ltd. , Beijing. May we suggest that you contact that company directly? We think the firm may be able to supply you with more quotations for a wider range of machines, including the knitting machines you requested.

Yours faithfully,

(2)

Dear Mr. ...

Automobile DVD Players

We are the manufacturers of BM cars and coaches. Our company is a subsidiary of BM Inc. of Houston, Texas. We are seeking an alternative supplier of automobile DVD players to equip our cars and coaches. As far as we know you do not have a local distributor of your products in this country.

A full specification of our requirements is given on the attached sheet.

Quantity required: 2500 sets

Delivery: by 20 April, 2009

Please quote us your best CIF Larado price, giving full specifications of your products.

We would need to have samples of the players to test in our laboratories before placing a firm order.

We usually deal with new suppliers on the basis confirmed irrevocable sight letter of credit.

If the laboratory tests are satisfactory and you can provide us with a good price and service, we will be happy to place more substantial orders on a regular basis.

We look forward to receiving an early reply to this enquiry.

Yours truly,

(Reply)

Dear Mr. ...

Thank you for your enquiry of March 4. We are actually very familiar with your automobiles and are pleased to inform you that we have a new model of DVD players that fits your specifications exactly.

The most suitable model is LN – 600. This product combines economy with stable performance. It is available now from stock. We are pleased to quote as follows:

Description: Automobile DVD players LN – 600

Quantity: 2500 sets

Price: USD290 per set CIF Larado

Payment: Confirmed, irrevocable sight L/C

This offer is firm, subject to your reply reaching here by March 25.

Enclosed please find a full specification of our products.

I have instructed our agent Mr. Lamont to deliver three samples to you next week, so that you can carry out the laboratory tests. Our own laboratory reports, enclosed with this letter, show that our new LN – 600 performs as well as any of our competitors' products and, in some respects, out – performs them.

If you would like any further information, please telephone or fax me: my phone number is 034 – 7713408.

I look forward to hearing from you.

Yours truly,

2. Non – Firm offer

(1)

Dear Mr. ...

We have just bought from the producers a large quantity of high quality rugs and carpets at low prices.

As you are one of our regular customers, we would like you to share in the excellent opportunity our purchase provides. We can offer you woolen carpets with traditional patterns in a variety of colors at prices ranging from $... to $... per square foot. These prices are 5% below current wholesale prices.

This is an exceptional opportunity for you to buy a stock of high – quality products at prices we cannot repeat and we hope you will take full advantage of it. If you are interested, please contact our representative in New York not later than Friday next, the 6th of March.

Sincerely,

(2)

Dear Sirs,

　　We are in receipt of your letter dated March 21 and, as requested, are airmailing you, under separate cover, one catalogue and two sample books for our Printed Shirting. We hope they will reach you in due course and will help you in making your selection.

　　In order to start a concrete transaction between us, we take pleasure in making you a special offer, subject to our final confirmation, as follows:

　　Art. No.：81000 Printed Shirting

　　Design No.：72435_ 2A

　　Specifications：30×36×72×69　　　　　35/6"×42yds

　　Quantity：18,000 yards

　　Packing：In bales or in wooden cases, at seller's option

　　Price：RMB… per yard CIFC5% Lagos

　　Shipment：to be made in three equal monthly installments, beginning from June, 2000.

　　Payment：By confirmed, irrevocable L/C payable by draft at sight to be opened 30 days before the time of shipment.

　　We trust the above will be acceptable to you and await with keen interest your trial order.

Yours faithfully,

三、信件主要内容

1. 询价函

（1）表达交易意向

● We believe there is a promising market here for handbags of high quality.

● We are very much interested in your most popular mobile phones in the latest range advertised in our local newspaper.

● After studying your leaflets, we are particularly interested in the following items:

（2）请对方提供一般交易条件或具体报价

● We would appreciate your sending us an illustrated catalogue and a price list of the phones advertised.

● We would like you to send us details of your various ranges, including sizes, colors and

prices, and also samples of the different qualities of leathers used.
- When replying, please state your terms of payment and discount you would allow on purchases of large quantities of individual items.
- Please quote us your best CIF Rotterdam prices for the above-mentioned items both on 20'FCL and LCL basis as well as your terms of shipment, payment and insurance.

2. 虚盘函

虚盘的内容与下一章要约函的内容基本相同,只是提出了保留条件。具体内容分别参见下一章以及本章重点用语中关于保留条件的提出。

四、重点用语

1. 表达购买意愿

(1) be interested in... 欲购……

(2) be in need of... 需购……

(3) be in the market for... 欲购……

① We are interested in your electric heaters, particularly Model F.

② As the season is rapidly coming, our buyers are badly in need of the goods.

③ We are in the market for general business application software for our clients.

2. 关于产品销路

(1) There is a demand for...(市场)对……有需求

(2) be in great demand(市场)对……需求量大

(3) a ready market 畅销

(4) sell well 畅销

① As there is a demand for cotton piece goods at our end, we will appreciate your quoting us lowest price.

② The pamphlet is in great demand.

③ Chinese Black Tea always finds a ready market in North America.

④ You can find a ready market for black tea here.

⑤ Tiantan Brand men's shirts enjoy a ready market in Kuwait.

⑥ Chinese Black Tea sells well in North America.

3. 请求报价

(1) quote *v.* 报价

   quotation *n.* 报价

(2) offer *v. n.* 报盘

① Please quote us your lowest price CIF London.

② Please quote your lowest price CIF London for your Printed Shirting.

③ Please quote the supply of 100 reams(令) of good quality poster paper(广告纸), inclusive of our 5% commission, stating the earliest date of shipment.

Please send us your lowest quotation CIF Hamburg for 10 metric tons of walnut meat.

Please send us by return mail your detailed offers for the following:

Please offer us 500 bicycles CIF London.

4. 提出保留条件

subject to the goods being unsold	以货未售出为准
subject to our final confirmation	以我方最终确认为准
subject to prior sale	以先售出为准
without engagement	不受约束

Owing to the usual shortage of stock, this offer is made subject to the goods being unsold.

In reply, we take pleasure in making you a special offer, subject to our final confirmation, as follows:

 课后练习

1. Translate the following sentences into English.

（1）本地区对中等价格的高品质手套有稳定的需求，请惠寄贵公司的手套目录一份，详述有关价目与付款条件，并惠赐样品。

（2）如果贵方能提供所要求型号和质量的 MP4 播放器，我方就可向贵方定期大量订货。

（3）如果贵公司能报 CIFC5% 上海最优惠价，并说明可立即装运的货物的各自数量和规格，我们将不胜感激。

（4）很高兴随信寄上最新的商品手册。贵公司也可以在网上订购，网址是：http://jacksonbro.com。

（5）在欧洲市场上，只有全棉床单有销路，任何化学合成纤维和混纺布料都不受欢迎。

（6）以上报价为 FOB 青岛价，包括包装成本，我方不受约束。

2. Write to Atlanta Nuts Co., asking for detailed information about the kind of nuts available at the moment and the terms and conditions for prompt delivery.

3. Write a letter to invite a firm offer for the following items on the seller's catalogue.

（1）第 12 号和第 81 号春装花式纽扣；

（2）FOB 中国港口价；

（3）标明最低出口起订量；

（4）请告知包装、重量、交货及其他必要细节。

第五章 要 约

在国际货物贸易中，要约是买方或卖方向对方提出的具体、肯定的订约建议。卖方无保留的报盘和买方的订单是常见的两种要约形式。其中买方订单也可能是对卖方要约的接受，视交易磋商的进程而定。

一、业务背景知识

要约的构成要件及法律效力

《联合国国际货物销售合同公约》第十四条至第十七条对要约的构成要件和约束力做出了规定。

第十四条

（1）向一个或一个以上特定的人提出的订立合同的建议，如果十分确定并且表明要约人在得到接受时承受约束的意旨，即构成要约。一个建议如果写明货物并且明示或暗示地规定数量和价格或规定如何确定数量和价格，即为十分确定。

（2）非向一个或一个以上特定的人提出的建议，仅应视为邀请做出要约，除非提出建议的人明确地表示相反的意向。

第十五条

（1）要约于送达受要约人时生效。

（2）一项要约，即使是不可撤销的，得予撤回，如果撤回通知于要约送达受要约人之前或同时，送达受要约人。

第十六条

（1）在未订立合同之前，要约得以撤销，如果撤销通知于受要约人发出接受通知之前送达受要约人。

（2）但在下列情况下，要约不得撤销：(a)要约写明接受的期限或以其他方式表明要约是不可撤销的，(b)受要约人有理由信赖该项要约是不可撤销的，而且受要约人已本着对该项要约的信赖行事。

第十七条

一项要约，即使是不可撤销的，于拒绝通知送达要约人时终止。

二、例信

1. Offers by the seller

(1)

Dear Mr. . . .

Thank you for your enquiry of March 8. We also confirm having received your sample.

We have carefully examined the sample and can assure you that we are able to produce articles of identical type and quality. Based on your annual requirement, we are making you the following offer:

Men's Box			
Calf Shoes (brown)	Sept.	100 pairs	£ 15.00 pr
_ ditto_ (black)	Immediate	100 pairs	£ 15.00 pr
Ladies' kid			
Tie Shoes	Sept.	100 pairs	£ 14.50 pr
Ladies Calf			
Court Shoes	Oct.	100 pairs	£ 14.00 pr
		Net price, FOB London	

All items for which we have quoted are made from very best quality leather and can be supplied in a range of designs and colours wide enough to meet the requirements of a fashionable trade such as yours.

We look forward to receiving your order.

Yours sincerely,

(2)

Dear Sirs,

Many thanks for the enquiry of 4 March 2009, reference MN/OI. We have pleasure in quoting as follows:

White 50/50 polyester/cotton mixture men's shirts as per sample, label No. 203, in assorted sizes between 35 and 44, individually packed in plastic bags and boxed in 100's no less than 50 of each size, packed in export crates of 1,000 shirts.

US $ 5.00 per shirt

EXW Textiles Building Richmond

Payment: By Irrevocable Letter of Credit opened in our favour with the Commercial Bank of Ruralia, Industrial Area Branch.

Quantity: Minimum order 1,000 shirts, maximum present capacity 10,000 shirts a month.

Delivery: Within 3 months of notification of receipt of Letter of Credit.

Validity: This quotation is firm for orders dispatched before 1 August 2009.

We hope that this meets with your approval. Please let us know if you require any further information or samples.

Yours sincerely,

2. Orders

(1)

Dear Sirs,

Your Reference LB/AP

We enclose our order No. 345 for four items in your latest catalogue.

We note that you can supply these items from stock and hope you will send them without delay.

Yours sincerely,

JB SIMPSON & CO. LTD.
18 Deansgate Blackpool
FY37JG

ORDER

July 4, 2009

<u>Order No. 345</u>

China National Textiles
IMP & EXP Corporation
Beijing
China

Please supply the following items in accordance with the terms and conditions of Order No. 344.

Qty	Item	Catalogue No.	Price (net)
23	Bed Sheets, 106cm, blue	75	US $ 5.00 each
25	– do. –, 120cm, pink	82	$ 6.00 each
5	Pillow Cases, blue	150	$ 1.50 each
50	– do. –, pink	162	$ 1.70 each

FOB China port

For JB Simpson & Co. Ltd.
W. James
Secretary

(2)

Gentlemen:

   We thank you for your quotation of August 15 together with patterns of Printed Shirting. We find both quality and prices satisfactory and are pleased to give you an order for the following items on the understanding that they will be supplied from stock at the prices named:

Quantity	Pattern No.	Prices
40,000yards	191	HK $ 11 per yd.
30,000yards	193	HK $ 14 per yd.
40,000yards	195	HK $ 18 per yd.

(All the prices are FOB HongKong)

   We expect to find a good market for the above and hope to place further and large orders with you in the near future.

   Our usual terms of payment are by D/P 60 days and we hope they will be satisfactory to you. Meanwhile, should you wish to make enquiries concerning our financial standing, you may refer to the following bank:

   … (name and address of the bank)

Yours truly,

(3)

Dear Sirs,

<u>Contract No. 78PGO17</u>
<u>Tiantan Brand Men's Shirts</u>

 We have received the captioned shipment ex S.S. "East Wind" and are very pleased to inform you that we find the goods quite satisfactory. As we believe we can sell additional quantities in this market, we wish to place with you a repeat order for 1,000 dozen of the same style and sizes. If possible, please arrange early shipment of this repeat order, as we are badly in need of the goods.

 In case the said goods are not available from stock, we shall be very grateful to you, if you will advise us as to the specifications of those which can be shipped from stock, stating full particulars.

Yours truly,

三、信件主要内容

1. 无保留的出口发盘函

(1) 确认收到询盘(若为主动报盘,该部分省略)

● Thank you for your enquiry of June 11 in which you asked about our porcelain(瓷,瓷器)ware.

● We were pleased to hear from your letter of 15th March that you were impressed with our selection of silk shirts.

● Thank you for your enquiry of August 10. We are pleased to tell you that we would be able to supply you with the high quality bicycles.

(2) 强调产品的优势特点——特别是与竞争对手相比的独特之处

● We think you have made an excellent choice in selecting this line, and once you have seen the samples we are sure you will agree that this is unique both in texture【(织物的)密度、质地】and colour.

● Once you have seen the machine in operation we know you will be impressed by its trouble-free performance.

● We can assure you that the Ultra 2008 is one of the most outstanding machines on the market today, and our confidence in it is supported by our three-year guarantee.

(3) 按客户要求发盘,列明主要交易条件

主要交易条件指规格、数量、包装、价格、交货和支付条件。CIF 报价还会加上保险。

● For the Fancy Brand AGT-4 garment sewing machine, the best price is USD 78.00 per

set FOB Shanghai.
- We confirm our price for the Automatic Dishwasher at US $211.00 per set CFR Nagoya.
- In reply to your enquiry of May 28, we have the pleasure of quoting on 100 dozen nylon stockings at US $18 a dozen CIF Singapore.
- The wheat is to be packed in new gunny bags of 100kgs, and each bag weights about 1.5kgs.
- The trip scissors are packed in boxes of one dozen each, 100 boxes to a carton.
- Our shipment terms are shipment within three months from receipt of L/C.
- Our usual terms of payment are by irrevocable L/C available by draft at sight.
- The insurance shall be effected by the seller covering the invoice value plus 10% against Institute Cargo Clauses (A).

如果报价是有期限的,也应明确表示。
- This offer is valid for ten days.
- The quotations are for acceptance within two weeks.
- This offer is firm subject to your reply reaching us within 10 days.

(4) 回复客户提出的其他问题和要求
- The sample you asked for will follow by separate post.
- Enclosed please find the copy you requested for the inspection report.

(5) 鼓励客户订货
- We look forward to an initial order, which will convince you of the high quality of our goods.
- As we have been receiving a rush of orders now, we would advise you to place your order as soon as possible.
- This favorable offer will not be repeated for some time, and we accordingly look forward to an early order from you.

2. 买方要约——订购函

(1) 说明订购要求

提出订购要求实际是买方提出的一项购买要约,可以是主动提出的,也可以是根据卖方的报价提出的。其法律效力与卖方报实盘相同。
- We find both quality and prices satisfactory and are pleased to give you an order for the following items on the understanding that they will be supplied from stock at the prices named: ...
- We thank you very much for your letter of 15th February with patterns and price lists. We have chosen three items for which we enclose Order No. 777.
- As we believe we can sell additional quantities in this market, we wish to place with you a repeat order for 1,000 dozen of the same style and sizes.

（2）提出交易条件

作为一项要约，订单的交易条件也必须明确具体，明示或暗示地规定主要的交易条件，一旦成交，便可作为交易的依据。主要包括：商品名称、品质规格、数量、价格等；此外还会规定付款方式、交货期等。

- Quantity   Pattern No.   Prices(net)
  500metres   64   US $0.95 per metre
  350metres   79   US $0.90 per metre
  400metres   83   US $1.00 per metre

  （All the prices are FOB Hong Kong）
- Packing：by standard export case of 120 cans each.
- Our usual terms of payment are by D/P 60 days and we hope they will be satisfactory to you.
- The goods are urgently required, so prompt delivery will be most appreciated.

（3）指示下一步行动或未来业务展望

- We expect to find a good market for these canned mushrooms and hope to place further and larger order with you in the near future.
- Please send us your confirmation of sales in duplicate.
- In case the said goods are not available from stock, we shall be very grateful to you, if you will advise us as to the specifications of those which can be shipped from stock, stating full particulars.

四、重点用语

1. 报盘

（1）Offer sth.

（2）Make sb. an offer for sth.

① We offer firm the following, usual terms.

② We make a firm offer for the following on usual terms.

③ We make you a firm offer subject to reply by 5 pm, our time, Wednesday, October 3.

④ We offer firm CIF, shipment within 30 days, subject to your reply reaching here by 10a.m., Tuesday, our time.

2. 订单和订购

（1）order   n. 订单，所定的货物；vt. 订购

（2）place an order with sb. for sth.   向某人订购某种产品

（3）repeat order   续订订单

      trial order   试订订单

      regular order   常规订单

      fresh order   新订单

例如：

We are pleased to place an order with you for garments.
We received an order for 2000 tons of beans.
We have large orders to fill.
Your order will be dispatched in a week.
They ordered a new production line from Switzerland.

 课后练习

1. Translate the following sentences into English：

（1）我方按要求报手捡不分级山东花生 250 吨，CFR 哥本哈根或其他欧洲主要口岸价，每公吨净价人民币 4 000 元，2009 年 10 月、11 月装运。

（2）随函寄上高品质照相机和镜头报价单。

（3）必须强调指出，由于供应有限、需求量大，该报盘有效期仅为一周。

（4）现报盘如下，以贵公司北京时间 5 月 12 日复到有效。

（5）我方对贵方提供的不同型号的 MP4 播放器感兴趣，并决定按贵公司信函中所述条件试订下列商品，但请保证本月底发货。

（6）6 月 5 日函及花式样和价目单均收到，谢谢。我们已选妥，并随附第 342 号订单。

2. Write and order for two of the items listed below, specifying quantity, unit price, total amount and terms of payment, asking for prompt shipment by parcel post.

Citrocomp 软件目录

品名	订货号码	价格
自动记分软件	123—456	US＄10.00
语法结构改错软件	531—024	＄24.00

3. Translate into English.

XX 先生，
　　贵公司 3 月 2 日关于 2 吨杏仁的询价单收到了，谢谢。现按上月所寄样品报价如下：
　　品名：甜杏仁（见样品）
　　等级：二级
　　数量：两公吨

价格：每吨 5000 美元 FOB 青岛

包装：纸箱装

交货：5/6 月

付款：信用证

因货源短缺，订单须于 3 月底前寄到，逾期无法供应，请谅解。

此致

4. Discuss whether or not the offers of first group of sample letters in this chapter can be canceled.

第六章 承诺、反要约与拒绝

对于一项要约，受要约人的反应无外三种：同意、提出实质性修改或表示拒绝。不同的回应，具有不同的法律后果。

受要约人同意一项要约，即是承诺；表示同意的通知到达要约人时承诺生效，合同成立。

受要约人对要约提出实质性修改，即为拒绝原要约，并提出新的要约。实质性修改指对有关货物价格、付款、货物质量和数量、交货地点和时间、一方当事人对另一方当事人的赔偿责任范围或解决争端等的添加或提出不同条件。

受要约人也可能就要约的某些条件提出异议，但不提出具体条件，而是邀请要约人做出新的要约；或者受要约人由于某些原因无法成交，从而拒绝整个要约。

一、业务背景知识

关于受要约人的回应是否构成承诺，以及承诺的法律效力，《联合国国际货物销售合同公约》第十八至二十三条做出了规定：

承诺的要件及法律效力

第十八条

（1）受要约人声明或做出其他行为表示同意一项要约，即是承诺。缄默或不行动本身不等于承诺。

（2）承诺于表示同意的通知送达要约人时生效。如果表示同意的通知在要约人所规定的时间内，如未规定时间，在一段合理的时间内，未曾送达要约人，承诺成为无效，但须适当地考虑到交易的情况，包括要约人所使用的通信方法的迅速程度。对口头要约必须立即接受，但情况有别者不在此限。

（3）但是，如果根据该项要约或依照当事人之间确立的习惯做法或惯例，受要约人可以做出某种行为，例如与发运货物或支付价款有关的行为，来表示同意，而无须向要约人发出通知，则承诺于该项行为做出时生效，但该项行为必须在上一款所规定的期间内做出。

第十九条

（1）对要约表示接受但载有添加、限制或其他更改的答复，即为拒绝该项要约并构成新要约。

（2）但是，对要约表示接受但载有添加或不同条件的答复，如所在的添加或不同条件在实质上并不变更该项要约的条件，除要约人在不过分迟延的期间内以口头或书面通知反对其间的差异外，仍构成承诺。如果要约人不做出这种反对，合同的条件就以该项要约的条件以及接受通知所载的更改为准。

（3）有关货物价格、付款、货物质量和数量、交货地点和时间、一方当事人对另一方当事人的赔偿责任范围或解决争端等的添加或不同条件，均视为在实质上变更要约的条件。

第二十条

（1）要约人在电报或信件内规定的承诺期间，从电报交发时刻或信上载明的发信日期起算，如信上未载明发信日期，则从信封上所载日期起算。要约人以电话、电传或其他快速通信方法规定的接受期间，从要约送到受要约人时起算。

（2）在计算承诺期间时，承诺期间内的正式假日或非营业日应计算在内。但是，如果承诺通知在承诺期间的最后一天未能送到要约人的地址，因为那天在要约人营业地是正式假日，则承诺期间应顺延至下一个营业日。

第二十一条

（1）逾期承诺仍有承诺的效力，如果要约人毫不迟延地用口头或书面将此种意见通知受要约人。

（2）如果载有逾期承诺的信件或其他书面文件表明，它是在传递正常、能及时送达要约人的情况下寄发的，则该项逾期承诺具有承诺的效力，除非要约人毫不迟延地用口头或书面通知受要约人：他认为要约已经失效。

第二十二条

承诺得以撤回，如果撤回通知于承诺原应生效之前或同时送达要约人。

第二十三条

合同于按照本公约规定对要约的承诺生效时订立。

二、例信

1. Acceptance to an offer

Dear Mr. ...

We accept your offer of March 7 and confirm our order for 100 metric tons of Groundnut Oil according to terms you stated. Our order sheet is enclosed.

We will apply for the letter of credit soon. Please arrange shipment in time.

Yours sincerely,

2. Acceptance to an order

（1）

Dear Mr. ...

We were very pleased to receive your Order No. 345 for bed sheets and pillow cases. We accordingly accept the order and shall arrange delivery as soon as possible.

We hope they will reach you in good time and that we may have further orders from you.

Yours sincerely,

(2)

Dear Mr. ...

We have booked your Order No. 237 for 100 pumping machines and are sending you herewith our Sales Confirmation No. BP – 103 in duplicate. Please sign and return one copy to us for our file.

It is understood that a letter of credit in our favor covering the above-mentioned goods, will be established immediately. We wish to point out that the stipulations in the relevant credit should strictly conform to the terms stated in our Sales Confirmation in order to avoid subsequent amendments. You may rest assured that we shall effect shipment with the least possible delay upon receipt of the credit.

We appreciate your cooperation and look forward to receiving your further orders.

Yours truly,

3. Counter-offer by the buyer

(1)

Dear Mr. ...

Thank you for your letter of 20th this month, offering us 5,000 kilograms of walnut meat at £ 5 per kilogram.

However, we regret that your price is rather high and not acceptable to our clients. Besides, there's keen competition from suppliers in South Korea and Thailand.

If you can reduce your price by 5%, we might come to business.

Considering the long-standing business relationship between us, we make you such a counter-offer. As the market is declining, we hope you will consider our counter-offer most favourably and reply as soon as possible.

Yours truly,

(2)

Dear Mr. ...

<u>Lenovo Color TV sets</u>

We have received your offer No. 008 offering us 2,000 sets of the subject goods.

In reply, we regret to inform you that our clients find your price much too high. Information indicates that some kinds of the above articles made in other countries have been sold here about 6% lower than that of yours.

We do not deny that the quality of your products is slightly better, but the difference in price should not be so big. To step up the trade, we counter offer FOB Shanghai as follows, subject to your reply here by 5 p.m. our time, May 15th:

US $ 250.00 per set for Art. No. AB212
US $ 225.00 per set for Art. No. AB212
US $ 200.00 per set for Art. No. AB212

As the market is of keen competition, we look forward to your immediate acceptance.

Yours sincerely,

(3)

Dear Mr. ...

We thank you for your quotation of March 3rd for 100 sets of Lenovo 2188 Color TV sets. We find your price and delivery date satisfactory, however, we would like you to change your payment terms.

Our past purchase of other household electrical appliances from you has been paid usually by confirmed, irrevocable sight letter of credit. Under this condition, the expense is too high, and the tie-up of our funds lasts about three months. At present, this matter is particularly outstanding owing to the tight financial condition and unprecedented high bank interest.

In view of our long business relations and our close cooperation, we suggest that you accept either "Cash against Documents on arrival of goods" or "Drawing on us at 60 days' sight".

Your early favorable reply will be highly appreciated.

Yours sincerely,

4. Counter-offer by the seller

(1)

Dear Mr. ...

We accept your order No. TR-89 for 2 tons of Fungus, but ask for two week's delay in shipment. As you probably know, the recent dockers' strike delayed our shipments from the Far East. However, the strike is over, and ships are being unloaded.

We sincerely regret any inconvenience you may have experienced, and are making every effort to speed up the delivery. Your order will be processed by June 10th.

Sincerely,

(2)

Dear Mr. ...

We very much regret that we shall not be able to accept your order for Christmas packs of dates as supplied in previous years.

We are sure you will appreciate that the rough weather this year has made it impossible to purchase supplies at economic prices. Moreover, such purchases as we have made were not packaged in the traditional way, but in cartons with polythene tops. The price, therefore, is 20% higher than last year's. Would you please reply at once if this interests you?

In view of our long business connections we will definitely keep supplies available for you if you place an order within seven days.

Yours sincerely,

(3)

Dear Sirs,

We refer to your fax of the 2nd, in which you asked for more favorable terms. We regret that at the present moment, we are unable to offer more than the terms agreed upon last year. Apart from the fact that our profit margin is already low, there is the additional problem of maintaining our retail prices at a competitive level.

We, nevertheless, are willing to give you a discount on larger orders and enclose a list of the lines with the appropriate discount against each one.

We hope that these generous discounts will bring about a substantial order.

We look forward to hearing from you soon.

Yours sincerely,

Dear Mr. ...

We are sorry to learn from your fax of 22nd August that you find our prices too high. We do our best to keep prices as low as possible without sacrificing quality. To this end we are constantly enquiring into new methods of making shoes.

Considering the quality of the shoes offered we do not feel that the prices we quoted are at all excessive, but bearing in mind the long-standing relationship between our firms, we have decided to offer you a special discount of 3% on an order exceeding £10,000. We make this allowance because we should like to continue to do business with you, but we must stress that it is the furthest we can go. We hope this revised offer will now enable you to place an order.

Yours sincerely,

5. Inviting a new offer

(1)

Dear Sirs,

We have received your quotation No. TY768 but regret to find the price irrelevant to current market trend.

Right now in Europe, there are more Asian sellers and more material from Eastern Europe. The chief sellers, worrying about their market shares, are again lowering their prices. In the circumstances, the FH Group must have good reasons to be ready to accept last year's price level.

According to our information, the FH Group tactic is to buy as much Chinese material as possible and pay a good price for it. Then they sell the Chinese material along with their own at the lower market price in Europe. Since their purchase from China is only a small part of their total sales, the cost of doing so is absorbed by the large profit margin of their own material. This means that when other competitors withdraw, Chinese suppliers will find it more difficult to sell and have to bow to the FH Group's pressure to let it dominate the market.

We hope you will reconsider the matter and send us a new offer.

Yours sincerely,

(2)

Dear Sirs,

We have carefully considered your counter-proposal of 5th May to our offer of woolen underwear, but very much regret that we cannot accept it. The prices we quoted in our letter of 2nd May leave us with only the smallest of margins, they are in fact lower than those of our competitors for goods of similar quality.

The wool used in the manufacture of our "Thermaline" range undergoes a special process that prevents shrinkage and increase durability. The fact that we are the largest suppliers of woolen underwear in this country is in itself evidence of the good value of our products.

If, having given further thought to the matter, you feel you cannot accept our offer, we hope it will not prevent you from approaching us on some other occasions. We shall always be glad to hear from you and will carefully consider any proposal likely to lead to business between us.

Yours sincerely,

Dear Sirs,

Thank you for your fax of 7th July enclosing your order for 8000 meters of 100 cm wide CWT silk.

We are sorry we can no longer supply this silk. Fashions constantly change and in recent years the demand for watered silk has fallen to such an extent that we have ceased to produce it.

In its place we can offer you our new "Gossamer" brand of rayon. This is a finely woven, hard wearing, non-creasable material with a most attractive luster. The large number of repeat orders we regularly receive from leading distributors and dress manufacturers is clear evidence of the popularity of this brand. At the low price of only £ 1.80 a meter this rayon is much cheaper than silk and its appearance is just as attractive.

We are makers of other kinds of cloth in which you may be interested and are sending you a full range of patterns by parcel post. All these are selling well in many countries and we can safely recommend them. We can supply all of them from stock and if you decide to place an order, we could meet it promptly.

Yours sincerely,

6. Declining the deal

(1)

Dear Mr. ...

Thank you for your quotation of February 19 for the supply of a quantity of strawboards and your sample.

We carefully considered your proposal. We appreciate the good quality of your products, but your prices are much higher than those we have previously paid for strawboards of the same quality. Regretfully, we have decided to place the order elsewhere.

Thank you for your trouble in this matter. We shall continue to place orders and will invite your quotation on this line in the future.

Sincerely,

(2)

Dear Mr. ...

We thank you for your Order No. 123 for 5 tons of White Fungus.

However, because our supply of raw materials has been committed to other orders for months in advance, we are unable to accept your order at this time. Please understand.

Yours truly,

三、信件主要内容

1. 接受函

(1) 明确表示接受对方要约，不附加保留条件

- We accept your counter-offer of March 8th and are pleased to confirm having concluded the transaction of the captioned goods with you.
- Thank you for your offer of May 5th. we are pleased to book with you an order for 100 metric tons of Groundnut Oil on terms of your offer.
- We accept your order of June 3rd, and will arrange shipment accordingly.
- Although your price is below our level, we accept, as an exception, your order with a view to initiating business with you.
- Thank you for your Order No. A-102, which you faxed to us yesterday. We are glad to tell you that all the items can be delivered by the end of May.
- We have received with thanks your order for 5 tons of White Fungus. We are working on your order and will keep you informed in time of the progress.

(2) 指示下一步行动———一般包括会签合同、安排装运、开证等

- Attached is our Sales Confirmation No. EX-15 in duplicate made out against your order mentioned above. Please countersign it and return one copy for our files, and establish the covering L/C in May 2005.
- Out order sheet is enclosed and the relative credit will be cabled to you within the next

few days.
- It is understood that a letter of credit in our favor covering the above-mentioned goods will be established immediately. We wish to point out that the stipulations in the relevant credit should strictly conform to the terms stated in our Sales Confirmation in order to avoid subsequent amendments.
- You may rest assured that we shall effect shipment with the least delay upon receipt of the credit.

（3）展望或推动未来业务
- We appreciate your cooperation and look forward to receiving your further orders.
- If this order is executed satisfactorily, we shall be happy to place further orders with you.
- As you may not be aware of the wide range of goods we deal in, we are enclosing a copy of our catalogue and hope that our handling of your first order with us will lead to further business between us and mark the beginning of a happy working relationship.
- It might interest you to know that the buyers concerned are among the leading importers of edible oils in this city, it is likely that they might want to duplicate their order before the month is out.

2. 反要约

（1）确认收到对方来函
礼节性地感谢对方来函，简洁地表明对对方来函的总体态度。
- We are glad to receive your letter of March 22nd but sorry to learn that your customers find our prices too high.
- In reply, we regret to say that your prices are not competitive enough.

（2）提出变更的交易条件，作进一步的解释说明
寻找适当的理由解释不能接受对方交易条件的原因，如市场总体行情、品质因素、利润、成本约束、汇率变动等。还盘的核心是理由的陈述。耐心、诚恳和有说服力的还盘理由是写好还盘的关键。
- We believe our prices are quite realistic; it is impossible that any other supliers can underquote us if their products are as good as ours in quality.
- The price we quoted is accurately calculated. We have cut the profit to the minimum in order to expand the market.
- Information here indicates that plush toys from other suppppliers sold about 5% lower than yours.

（3）提出新的交易条件（价格、数量、交货期、付款方式等）
- In order to assist you to compete with other dealers in the market, we have decided to reduce 2% of the price quoted to you previously, if your order reaches 5000 sets at one time.
- We can give you 3% allowance if you agree to pay 10% of the order value by T/T in ad-

vance.

- If we receive your order within the next ten days, we will give priority to it for May shipment.

（4）期待对方回复

- We hope you will agree to our suggestions and look forward to receiving a trial order from you.
- We will appreciate it if you will consider our new offer favorably and fax us your acceptance as soon as possible.

总之，反要约的关键在于以适当的理由，从适当的角度提出各种新条件，以促成早日成交。毫无说明的修改和拒绝都是不可取的。

四、重点用语

交易洽谈过程中，品质、数量、包装、价格、支付、运输、保险等，都是讨论的内容，其他条件在以后的章节中交代，本章介绍讨论价格的用语。

1. 关于价格水平

- on the high/low side　　偏高/低

We note from your letter of May 30 that the price offered by us for the subject article is found to be on the high side.

- out of line　　与……不一致

  in line　　与……一致

  Your price is out of line with the prevailing market level.

  Your price is quite in line.

- competitive price　　有竞争力的价格

  keen price　　克己价格

  favorable price　　优惠价格

  realistic price　　符合实际的价格

  moderate price　　适中的价格，公道的价格

  reasonable price　　合理的价格

- 价格飞涨

  The price shoots up.

  The price goes up abnormally.

  The price rises abnormally.

- 价格猛跌

  The price falls suddenly.

  The price goes down with a run.

  The price slumps.

  The price declines heavily.

- 减价

    reduce price

    cut down price

    lower price

    shade(略减) price

    bring down price

    If you can reduce your limit by, say 3%, we might come to terms.

    There is no possibility of our cutting the price to the extent you indicated, i.e. 8%.

2. 有关市场行情

Market is dull.	市场呆滞
Market is easy.	市场疲软
Market is weak.	市场疲软
Market is declining.	行市下跌
Market is strong.	行市坚挺
Market is advancing.	行市上涨
Market is firm.	行市坚挺
Market is brisk.	行市活跃

3. 折扣与佣金

- give discount/allowance

    grant discount/allowance

    make allowance

    offer discount

    We shall place an order with you, provided you make some allowance on quoted price.

    On an order exceeding $10,000, we allow 10% discount off the price.

    The goods are sold at a discount of 20% off recent prices.

- allow commission　　给予佣金

    draw commission　　提取佣金

    We are willing to allow you commission at 10% calculated on gross profit.

    We allow them a commission of 3%.

    We draw a commission of 3% on each sale.

 课后练习

1. Translate the following sentences into English.

(1) 近期原材料成本上涨,如按你公司所提减价15%,将大大影响产品的质量标准。

(2) 订单超过300件(包括300件),我们给予4%特别折扣,希望收到贵公司订单。

(3) 我们的价格已经充分考虑了大宗订单的因素。如你所知,我们在激烈竞争的市场上经营，被迫将价格降到最低。我们希望能够降价，但无能为力。

（4）由于出口计价货币美元最近大幅贬值，我们很遗憾不得不宣布，从5月1日起出口价格上升10%。

（5）我们希望确认，经过最近几次往来函电，与贵公司达成30吨花生仁交易。

（6）随函附上标题合同正本一式两份，其中一份请会签并寄还我方，以供存档。

2. Translate the following letter into English.

XX先生：
　　我们确认收到贵公司维生素C的第PL—23号订单，交货期为六、七月。
　　我公司将按照双方协议的时间表，根据我公司4月19日报价中所列条件进行发货。
　　希望这批订货能使贵方满意，并盼今后不断向我订货。
　　此致
敬礼

3. Order for computers from your customer cannot be met because the goods are out of stock. Write to express your regrets and explain why.

第七章 合 同 书

  关于货物买卖合同的形式,《联合国国际货物销售合同公约》没有特殊的要求,口头、书面的都可以。其中书面形式包括合同书、信件和数据电文。当事人订立合同,并非必须采用书面的形式,更无须一定签署专门的合同书。

  我国在加入《联合国国际货物销售合同公约》时,提出两项保留,其中之一就是关于书面形式的规定。《中华人民共和国合同法》关于合同形式的规定,基本精神是尊重当事人的意思自治,当事人约定采用书面形式的,应采用书面形式;当事人采用合同书形式的,双方当事人签字或盖章时合同成立。

  实际业务中,买卖双方口头达成交易后,往往还要书面确认,此时的确认函,应为合同成立的证明。有时,口头或书面达成一致后,还约定签订正式合同书,或会签卖方的售货确认书。此时,合同成立的时间和地点,适用《联合国国际货物销售合同公约》与适用《中华人民共和国合同法》会有不同解释。

  本章介绍口头合同的书面确认函,以及合同书。同时对国际货物买卖的主要条款逐一介绍,范例合同中的一般性条款体现了国际货物买卖相关内容的习惯做法。

一、业务背景知识

1. 《联合国国际货物销售合同公约》对合同形式的规定

第十一条

销售合同无须以书面订立或书面证明,在形式方面也不受任何其他条件的限制。销售合同可以用包括人证在内的任何方法证明。

2. 《中华人民共和国合同法》关于合同形式的规定

第十条

当事人订立合同,有书面形式、口头形式和其他形式。

法律、行政法规规定采用书面形式的,应当采用书面形式。当事人约定采用书面形式的,应当采用书面形式。

第十一条

书面形式是指合同书、信件和数据电文(包括电报、电传、传真、电子数据交换和电子邮件)等可以有形地表现所载内容的形式。

第三十二条

当事人采用合同书形式订立合同的,自双方当事人签字或盖章时合同成立。

第三十三条

当事人采用信件、数据电文等形式订立合同的,可以在合同成立之前要求签订确认书。签订确认书时合同成立。

第三十五条

当事人采用合同书形式订立合同的，双方当事人签字或者盖章的地点为合同成立的地点。

第三十六条

法律、行政法规规定或者当事人约定采用书面形式订立合同，当事人未采用书面形式但一方已经履行主要义务，对方接受的，该合同成立。

第三十七条

采用合同书形式订立合同，在签字或者盖章之前，当事人一方已经履行主要义务，对方接受的，该合同成立。

二、例信

1. Acknowledging an order

Dear Sirs,

We thank you for your quotation of 3rd October and the sample garments you sent us. We find both quality and prices satisfactory and are pleased to place an order with you for the following:

1,000　MJ Blouses

（five colors and five sizes）

2,000　CP Sun tops

（also five colors and five sizes）

The terms agreed upon with Mr. Wang during my telephone conversation this morning are as follows:

a. prices as stated in your quotation of 3rd October to include delivery to final destination.

b. payment to be made in Sterling to your London representative within one month of the arrival of the goods at Liverpool.

c. Insurance to be arranged by you with a Lloyd's broker through your London representative.

We should appreciate prompt shipment and hope to establish a regular connection for the future if this first consignment proves to conform to the samples supplied.

Yours sincerely,

2. Seller's confirmation

Dear Sirs,

We wish to refer to the recent exchange of cables and are pleased to confirm having concluded with you a transaction of 30 metric tons of groundnut kernels.

Enclosed is our Sales Confirmation No. 345 in duplicate. Please countersign and return one copy to us for our file. We trust you will open the relative L/C at an early date.

As regards additional quantities, we are working and will let you have an offer sometime next week.

Yours faithfully,

3. Sales Contract

SALES CONTRACT   No.

Date:

Signed at:

The Buyer: The Seller:

Hereby the Buyers agree to buy and the Sellers agree to sell the commodities on the terms and conditions stipulated below:

Article Number:

Description:

Quantity:

Unit Price:

Amount:

Goods:

With % more or less both in amount and quantity allowed at the Sellers option.

Total Value & Terms:

Packing and Shipping Mark:

Time of shipment:

Loading Port & Destination:

Insurance:

Terms of Payment:

Remarks:

The Buyers shall sign/counter sign one copy of this contract and return it to the Sellers within ____ days after receipt. Contract No. and only brief names of commodity are required to be quoted in the covering L/C.

General Terms:

1. If the commodities contracted herein are hand-made, some deviations in specifications and pattern shall be allowed, while for those made of natural materials, variation in shades, tints, etc. are acceptable.

2. The Seller shall not be responsible for late or non-delivery of goods in the event of force majeure of any contingencies beyond Seller's control.

3. Claims if any, concerning the goods shipped shall be filed within 30 days after arrival at destination supported by an inspection report. It is understood that the Sellers shall not be liable for any discrepancy of the goods shipped due to causes for which the Insurance Company, other transport organization or Post Office are liable.

4. This Contract shall become effective once mutually signed. Neither modification nor cancellation is allowed unless otherwise agreed upon by both parties.

5. All disputes arising from the execution of, or in connection with this Contract, shall be settled amicably through friendly consultation. In case no settlement can be reached there from, the case under dispute shall then be submitted to the China Council for the Promotion of International Trade, Beijing for arbitration in accordance with its Provisional Rules of Procedure. The arbitral award is final and binding upon both parties.

三、合同书的主要内容

国际货物买卖合同书的内容主要分为三部分：

1. 约首

约首通常包括：合同名称、合同编号、缔约依据、日期和地点、当事人的名称和地址。有的合同在约首还以序言的形式说明订约意图。

2. 本文

本文是合同的主要部分，一般以合同条款的形式具体列明交易的各项条件，规定双方当事人的权利和义务。它包括的内容主要有：货物名称、规格、数量；商品的包装和双方谈妥的价格；交付货物的时间、装运地和目的地；货物的运输保险由哪一方负责办理，保险险别、保险金额与所适用的保险条款；货款支付的时间和方式等。

此外，合同书中还包括一些预防与处理争议的条款，通常作为合同的一般交易条件列明在合同的备注栏或合同的背面。

3. 约尾

约尾是合同的结束部分，通常包括：合同所使用的文字及其效力、合同的份数、缔约人签字、合同生效时间和条件以及合同所适用的法律等。

四、合同书的主要条款示例

1. 品名及规格(Commodity Name and Specifications)

它是构成商品说明的重要组成部分,也是交易双方在交接货物时对货物品质界定的主要依据。商品的品质可以以实物或文字说明表示。有时可以加列品质机动幅度条款,即允许卖方交付货物的品质在一定范围内机动,从而有利于生产加工和合同履行。

- S312 16cm Christmas bear with cap and scarf, details as per the samples dispatched by the seller on 20th August 2008.
- Wilson Brand Football, Article Number WS 18, Size 5, Genuine Leather, Hand Sewn, FIFA Approved.
- Green Bean, Moisture 15% max, Admixture 1% max.

2. 数量(Quantity)

包括计量单位、商品数量或者再加上关于数量机动幅度的规定。

- 800 metric tons, 5% more or less at seller's option.

3. 包装(Packing)

包装条款主要包含的要素有:包装方式、外包装的种类及总件数,涉及集装箱数量时一般也会明确指出。

- 20 pieces to a box, 10 boxes to an export carton. Total 500 cartons in one 20 feet container.
- Each to be wrapped with paper then to a polybag, every dozen to a new strong wooden case, suitable for long voyage and well protected against dampness, moisture, shock, rust and rough handling. Total 500 wooden cases in one 40'FCL.

4. 价格(Price)

价格条款包括:各货号的单价(U-nit Price)、总值(Total Amount/Total Value)及合同总金额的大、小写等。其中,单价由计价货币、金额、数量单位和贸易术语四部分组成。

- USD 14,860.00 PER PC. CIFNEW YORK
-

UNIT PRICE	QUANTITY	AMOUNT
USD 125 PER PC. CIF NEW YORK	1000PC.	USD125,000.00
	LESS 2% DISCOUNT	USD2,500.00
	TOTAL	USD122,500.00

5. 装运(Shipment)

装运条款主要包括装运时间、装运港/地、目的港/地,以及分批转船等附加条件。

- Shipment from Shanghai to Genoa during July 2008 with partial shipments allowed.
- Shipment during June/July/August 2008 in three equal monthly lots.
- Shipment from Shanghai to Los Angeles with transshipment at Hongkong by Maersk Shipping Company.

有时,卖方为了防止因某些特殊情况延误装运而产生的违约行为,会在合同中对装运期限提出一些附加条件以保障其利益。如:

- Shipment within 30 days after receipt of L/C.
- Shipment during August 2008 subject to shipping space available.
- Shipment by the end of May 2008 subject to export license available by the seller.

6. 保险(Insurance)

以 CIF、CIP 作为贸易术语的合同中,保险条款是合同的主要条款之一。通常保险条款包含的要素有:何方办理保险,保险金额,保险险别,按什么保险条款保险。

- Insurance:To be covered by the Seller for 110% of total invoice value against All Risks and War Risks as per and subject to the relevant ocean marine cargo clauses of the People's Insurance Company of China dated 1/1/1981.
- Insurance:To be covered by the Seller for CIF value plus 10% against Institute Cargo Clauses A and Institute War Clauses(Cargo) dated 1/1/1982.

7. 支付(Payment)

合同中的支付条款根据不同的结算方式而内容各异。

- 汇付(Remittance)

The buyer shall pay 100% of the contract value to the seller in advance by T/T within 30 days after signing the contract.

The buyer shall pay the total contract value by T/T upon receipt of the original Bill of Lading sent by the seller.

- 跟单托收(Documentary Collection)

Upon first presentation the buyer shall pay against documentary draft at sight drawn by the seller. The shipping documents are to be delivered against payment only.

Upon first presentation the buyer shall duly accept the documentary draft at 30 days after sight drawn by the sellers and make the payment at its maturity. The shipping documents are to be delivered against payment only.

- 跟单信用证(Documentary Letter of Credit)

使用跟单信用证进行结算时,在合同的支付条款中应明确规定开证申请人、开证银行、开证时间、信用证种类、信用证金额、信用证到期地点和到期日等。

> The buyer shall open through a bank acceptable to the seller an irrevocable letter of credit payable at 45 days' sight for 100% of the contract value to reach the seller 30 days before the month of shipment and valid for negotiation in China until the 15th day after the date of shipment.

8. 预防与处理争议的条款(Disputes)

除了以上主要条款外,为在合同履行中尽量减少争议,或者在发生争议时能妥善解决,在国际货物买卖合同中通常还需要订立一些有关预防与处理争议的条款,主要包括检验条款、索赔条款、不可抗力条款和仲裁条款。

● 检验条款示例

It is mutually agreed that the Inspection Certificate of Quality and Quantity issued by the China Entry-Exit Inspection and Quarantine Bureau at the port of shipment shall be part of the documents to be presented for negotiation under the relevant L/C. The Buyer shall have the right to re-inspect the Quality and Quantity of the cargo. The re-inspection fee shall be borne by the Buyers. Should the Quality and/or Quantity be found not in conformity with that of the contract, the Buyers are entitled to lodge with the Sellers a claim which should be supported by survey reports issued by an independent public surveyor approved by the Sellers.

● 索赔条款示例

In case of quality discrepancy, claims should be filed by the Buyers within 30 days after the arrival of the goods at port of destination; while for quantity discrepancy, claims should be filed by the Buyers within 15 days after the arrival of the goods at port of destination. It is understood that the Sellers shall not be liable for any discrepancy of the goods shipped due to causes for which the insurance company, shipping company, other transportation organizations and/or the post office are liable.

● 不可抗力条款示例

If the fulfillment of the contract is prevented by reason of war or other causes of force majeure, which exists for three months after the expiring of the contract, the non-shipment of this contract is considered to be void, for which neither the Seller nor the Buyer shall be liable.

● 仲裁条款示例

Arbitration: All disputes in connection with this contract or the execution thereof shall be settled friendly through negotiations. In case no settlement can be reached, the case may then be submitted for arbitration to China International Economic and Trade Arbitration Commission in accordance with the provisional Rules of Procedures promulgated by the said Arbitration Commission. The arbitration shall take place in Shanghai and the decision of the Arbitration Commission shall be final and binding upon both parties. Arbitration fee shall be borne by the losing party. Or arbitration may be settled in the third country mutually agreed upon by both parties.

 课后练习

Translate the following contract into English.

合　同

日期：
合同号码：

买方：General Trading Company
卖方：天津轻工业进出口公司

经双方同意，按照下列条款买卖以下商品：

1) 商品名称："飞鸽"牌自行车
2) 规格：MB28 型
3) 数量：1 000 辆
4) 单价：每辆 70 美元，CIF 纽约
5) 总金额：70 000 美元（大写：柒万美元整）
6) 包装：木箱装
7) 唛头：由卖方决定
8) 保险：由卖方按 110% 发票金额投保一切险和战争险。
9) 装运期：不迟于 2008 年 3 月 31 日，允许分批和转船。
10) 装运港：中国港口
11) 目的港：纽约
12) 支付条款：即期信用证支付，信用证于装运期前一个月开至卖方，最晚装运期限后 15 天之内在中国议付有效。
13) 索赔：货到目的港 45 天内如发现货物品质、规格和数量与合同不符，除属于保险公司或船方责任外，买方有权凭卖方认可的独立检验机构出具的检验证书向卖方索赔、换货。
14) 不可抗力：由于人力不可抗拒的原因发生在制造、装载货运输过程中导致卖方延期交货或不能交货者，卖方可免除责任。在不可抗力发生后，卖方须立即电告买方及在 14 天之内以空邮方式向买方提供事故发生的证明文件。
15) 仲裁：凡有关执行合同所发生的一切争议应通过友好协商解决，如协商不能解决，则将分歧提交中国国际贸易促进委员会按有关仲裁程序进行仲裁，仲裁裁决将是终局的，双方均受其约束，仲裁费用由败诉方承担。

本合同 2008 年 2 月 5 日于天津签订。

买方　　　　　　　　　　　　　　　　　　卖方

（签名）　　　　　　　　　　　　　　　　（签名）

第五单元　合同的履行

合同履行过程中，需要买卖双方及时沟通信息、协调行动的环节主要是：①涉及货物交接的指派运输工具、发货，以及若需买方投保买方、卖方安排运输时，投保与发货的衔接等；②涉及支付的信用证开证、改证；所有支付方式下都存在的提交单据与付款。

因此，本单元分为两章，分别介绍以上环节买卖双方的往来信函，在支付环节还涉及与相关银行的往来信函。

规范买卖双方货物交接权利与义务的国际公约与国际惯例主要有：《联合国国际货物销售合同公约》的相关规定；国际商会的《国际贸易术语解释通则》。国际贸易支付中普遍遵循的国际惯例有：国际商会的《跟单信用证统一惯例》与《托收统一规则》。

各国国内立法一般都规定国际条约优先适用以及国际惯例的补缺原则。例如，我国《民法通则》第一百四十二条第二款规定："中华人民共和国缔结或参加的国际条约同中华人民共和国民事法律有不同规定的，适用国际条约的规定，但中华人民共和国声明保留的条款除外。"该条第三款规定："中华人民共和国法律或中华人民共和国缔结或参加的国际条约没有规定的，可以适用国际惯例。"

国际惯例虽然理论上不具备强制约束力，但由于得到相关参与方的广泛引用，成为事实上的法律。

在涉及相关内容时，本单元也将简单介绍这些公约与惯例的基本精神。

第八章 运输与保险

一、背景知识介绍

国际货物贸易的买卖双方适用贸易术语来规定双方在货物交接过程中各自承担的风险、费用和责任，并由此表示商品价格的构成因素。

国际商会制定的《国际贸易术语解释通则》（Incoterms），是全球普遍接受的国际贸易术语解释惯例。该《通则》经过1936、1953、1980、1990、2000多次修改版本，并于2010年推出最新的修改版本。同时2000版本仍可继续引用。如果想在合同中使用国际贸易术语解释通则2010，则应在合同中用类似词句做出明确表示，如"所选用的国际贸易术语，包括指定地点，标明国际贸易术语解释通则2010"。举例：FCA 34 Dongfang Road, Shanghai, China Incoterms® 2010，其中"FCA"是贸易术语，"34 Dongfang Road, Shanghai, China"是地址或地点，"Incoterms® 2010"表示引用2010通则。

在双方货物交接具体权利义务的变化上，Incoterms® 2010 与 Incoterms® 2000 比，主要是有：①将FOB、CFR、CIF三种贸易术语风险转移的界限由原来的"以装运港船舷为界"，改为"货物交到船上时"。②并且，考虑到《伦敦保险协会货物险条款》的修订，Incoterms® 2010 将与保险相关的信息义务纳入涉及运输合同和保险合同的A3和B3条款。这些规定已从 Incoterms® 2000 的A10和B10泛泛的条款中抽出。为了明确双方与保险相关义务，A3和B3中有关保险的用语也做了相应调整。

1. 主要贸易术语国际货物运输与保险手续办理责任，费用与风险的划分

这里简单介绍六种常用的国际贸易术语：FCA、CPT、CIP、FOB、CFR、CIF 中买卖双方运输、保险手续办理、费用分担、相关的通知义务以及风险划分。其中，FCA、CPT、CIP 适用于任何运输方式或多种运输方式，FOB、CFR、CIF 适用于海运及内河水运。

（1）运输、保险手续的办理与费用承担

● FCA（货交承运人）

卖方义务	买方义务
A3 运输合同与保险合同 a) 运输合同 卖方对买方无订立运输合同的义务。但若买方要求，或依商业实践，且买方未适时做出相反指示，卖方可以按照通常条件签订运输合同，由买方负担风险和费用。 b) 保险合同 卖方对买方无订立保险合同的义务。但应买方要求并由其承担风险和费用，卖方必须向买方提供后者取得保险所需信息。	B3 运输合同与保险合同 a) 运输合同 除了卖方按照 A3a) 签订运输合同情形外，买方必须自付费用签订自指定的交货地点起运货物的运输合同。 b) 保险合同 买方对卖方无订立保险合同的义务。
A4 交货 卖方必须在约定的日期或期限内，在指定地点或指定地点的约定点，将货物交给买方指定的承运人或其他人。	B4 收取货物 当货物按照 A4 交付时，买方必须收取。
A7 通知买方 由买方承担风险和费用，卖方必须就其已经按照 A4 交货或买方指定的承运人或其他人未在约定时间内收取货物的情况给予买方充分的通知。	B7 通知卖方 买方必须通知卖方以下内容： a) 按照 A4 所指定的承运人或其他人的姓名，以便卖方有足够时间按照该条款交货； b) 如适用时，在约定的交付期限内所选择的由指定的承运人或其他人收取货物的时间； c) 指定人使用的运输方式；及 d) 指定地点内的交货点。

● CPT（运费付至）

卖方义务	买方义务
A3 运输合同与保险合同 a) 运输合同 卖方必须签订或取得运输合同，将货物自交货地内的约定交货点运至指定目的地或该目的地的交付点。必须按照通常条件订立合同，由卖方支付费用，经由通常航线和习惯方式运送货物。如果双方没有约定特别的点或该点不能由惯例确定，卖方则可选择最适合其目的的交货点和指定目的地内的交货点。	B3 运输合同与保险合同 a) 运输合同 买方对卖方无订立运输合同的义务。

卖方义务	买方义务
b)保险合同 与 FCA 相同	b)保险合同 与 FCA 相同
A4 交货 卖方必须在约定的日期或期限内,以将货物交给按照 A3 签订的合同承运人方式交货。	B4 收取货物 当货物按照 A4 交付时,买方必须收取,并在指定目的地自承运人收取货物。
A7 通知买方 卖方必须向买方发出已按照 A4 交货的通知。卖方必须向买方发出任何所需通知,以便买方采取收取货物通常所需要的措施。	B7 通知卖方 当有权决定发货时间和/或指定目的地或目的地内收取货物的点时,买方必须向卖方发出充分的通知。

● CIP(运费和保险费付至)

卖方义务	买方义务
A3 运输合同与保险合同 a)运输合同 与 CPT 规定相同 b)保险合同 卖方必须自付费用取得货物保险。该保险需至少符合《协会货物保险条款》"条款 C"或类似条款的最低险别。保险合同应与信誉良好的承保人或保险公司订立。应使买方或其他对货物有可保利益者直接向保险公司索赔。当买方要求且能够提供卖方所需的信息时,卖方应办理任何附加险别,由买方承担费用。 保险最低金额是合同规定价格另加 10%,并采用合同货币。	B3 运输合同与保险合同 a)运输合同 与 CPT 规定相同 b)保险合同 买方对卖方无订立保险合同的义务。
A4 交货 与 CPT 相同	B4 收取货物 与 CPT 相同
A7 通知买方 与 CPT 相同	B7 通知卖方 与 CPT 相同

● FOB(船上交货)

卖方义务	买方义务
A3 运输合同与保险合同 a)运输合同 与 FCA 相同	B3 运输合同与保险合同 a)运输合同 除了卖方按照 A3a)签订运输合同情形外,买方必须自付费用签订自指定的装运港起运货物的运输合同。
b)保险合同 与 FCA 相同	b)保险合同 与 FCA 相同

A4 交货	B4 收取货物
卖方必须在指定装运港的装船点,以将货物置于买方指定的船上方式,或以取得已在船上交付的货物的方式交货。在其中任何情形下,卖方都必须在约定日期或期限内,按照该港的习惯方式交货。 如果买方没有指定特定的装货点,卖方则可在指定装运港选择最适合其目的的装货点。	当货物按照 A4 交付时,买方必须收取。
A7 通知买方	B7 通知卖方
由买方承担风险和费用,卖方必须就其已经按照 A4 交货或船舶未在约定时间内收取货物的情况给予买方充分的通知。	买方必须通知卖方以下内容: a)买方必须就船舶名称、装船点和其在约定期间内选择的交货时间,向卖方发出充分的通知。

● CFR(成本加运费)

卖方义务	买方义务
A3 运输合同与保险合同 a)卖方必须签订或取得运输合同,将货物自交货地的约定交货点运送至指定目的港或该目的港的交货点。必须按照通常条件订立合同,由卖方支付费用,经由通常航线,由通常用来运输该类商品的船舶运输。 b)保险合同 卖方对买方无订立保险合同的义务。但应买方要求并由其承担风险和费用,卖方必须向买方提供后者取得保险所需的信息。	B3 运输合同与保险合同 a)买方对卖方无订立运输合同的义务。 b)保险合同 买方对卖方无订立保险合同的义务。但应卖方要求,买方必须向卖方提供取得保险所需的信息。
A4 交货 卖方必须以将货物装上船,或者以取得已装船货物的方式交货。在其中任何情况下,卖方都必须在约定日期或期限内,按照该港的习惯方式交货。	B4 收取货物 当货物按照 A4 交付时,买方必须收取,并在指定的目的港自承运人收取货物。
A7 通知买方 卖方必须向买方发出所需的通知,以便买方采取收取货物通常所需要的措施。	B7 通知卖方 当有权决定货物运输时间和/或指定目的港内收取货物点时,买方必须向卖方发出充分的通知。

● CIF(成本、保险费加运费)

卖方义务	买方义务
A3 运输合同与保险合同 a)运输合同 同 CFR。 b)保险合同 同 CIP。	B3 运输合同与保险合同 a)运输合同 同 CFR。 b)保险合同 同 CIP。
A5 交货 同 CFR。	B5 收取货物 同 CFR。
A7 通知买方 同 CFR。	B7 通知卖方 同 CFR。

(2) 货物交接过程中风险的划分

FCA、CPT、CIP 贸易术语，货物灭失或损坏的风险在双方约定的地点货交承运人时转移至买方；FOB、CFR、CIF 贸易术语，风险在货物交到装运港船上时转移。承运人在 FCA、FOB 贸易术语下是买方指定的；在 CPT、CIP、CFR、CIF 贸易术语下是卖方指定的。

但是当买方没有履行通知义务，在 FCA、FOB 贸易术语下未通知卖方指定承运人等；CPT、CIP、CFR、CIF 贸易术语下有权决定发货时间和/或指定目的地或目的地内收取货物的点时，买方未给予卖方充分的通知。或 FCA、FOB 贸易术语下由买方办理运输时，承运人未在约定时间接管货物。买方从约定的交货日期或交货期限届满之日起，承担货物灭失或损坏的一切风险，但以该货物已清楚地确定为合同项下之货物为限。

2. 运输、保险单据的处理与相关权利的转移

(1) 海运提单与物权转移

提单在法律上具有物权证书的作用。船货抵达目的港后，承运人应向提单的合法持有人交付货物。提单可以通过背书转让，从而转让货物的所有权。

在国际货物贸易中，"空白抬头、空白背书"的提单是使用最多的一种提单，即提单的收货人栏内填写"凭指示"(To order)；再由托运人(卖方)空白背书。提单经过空白背书，成为不记名提单，即凭提单提货的凭证。

在信用证和托收结算方式下，卖方得到银行或买方的付款或付款保证的情况下，交出代表物权的提单；买方则在付款或保证付款后，得到提单，凭以提货。相反，如果银行或买方拒付，卖方保留对提单项下物权的控制，可以自行提货，或转让提单。

"空白抬头、空白背书"的提单，保证了物权转移与货款收付相互制约。

(2) 航空与铁路运输中交货与付款的制约

国际贸易中的航空运单和铁路运单与海运提单有很大不同，不具有物权凭证的性质，无法通过一手付款一手交单的方式实现物权、货款交接的制约。它们是承运人签发的收据，也是承托双方的运输合同。但是二者均不可转让，在运单的收货人栏内，必须详细填写收货人的全称和地址，而不能做成指示性抬头。

国际铁路联运运单正本随同货物到达终到站，并交给收货人，它既是铁路承运货物出具的凭证，也是铁路与货主交接货物、核收运杂费和处理索赔与理赔的依据。运单副本于运输合同缔结后交给发货人，是卖方凭以向收货人结算货款的主要证件。

航空运单正本一式三份，每份都印有背面条款，其中第一份交发货人，是承运人或其代理人接收货物的依据；第二份由承运人留存，作为记账凭证；第三份随货同行，在货物到达目的地，交付给收货人时作为核收货物的依据。

因此，在航空与铁路运输中，货物一旦发运，卖方便无法通过控制货运单据控制货物。对于资信没有十分把握的客户，要使用信用证方式结算。必要时可指定目的地代理，以目的地代理作为运单的收货人。

(3) CIF、CIP 贸易术语交易中国际货运险保险单据与索赔权转移

国际货物运输保险的保险单是可以背书转让的单据，即被保险人可以通过背书的方

式，将保险单赋予的损害赔偿请求权及相应的诉讼权转让给受让人。

CIF、CIP 贸易术语的交易，卖方负责办理国际货物运输保险手续。一般做法是：保险单中的被保险人填写为卖方，再由卖方经过空白背书，转让保险单的权利。卖方将保险单与其他结算单据一起通过银行提交买方，买方付款或承诺付款后得到单据，取得单据权利。

投保时卖方对被保险货物具有可保利益，根据 Incoterms® 2010，卖方承担货物在指定装运港装上船（或按 Incoterms® 2000，以装运港船舷为界）、或货交承运人之前灭失或损坏的风险。但是从货物在装运港装上船（或按 Incoterms® 2000，以装运港船舷为界）、或货交承运人之后整个运输途中货物灭失或损坏的风险由买方承担，买方拥有可保利益。

这样做既符合被保险人是保险利益的所有者的原则，又可以保证卖方在得到买方或银行付款之前拥有或自由转让保险单赋予的权利。如果在卖方尚未收妥货款的情况下以买方作为"被保险人"，有较大的风险。一旦碰到买方拒付货款，或是信用证项下出现单证不符而遭到拒付的情况，恰遇货物在海运途中发生保险范围内的损失，卖方则无法凭该保险单向保险公司提出索赔。不仅如此，由于保险单据的被保险人是买方，卖方想要转让货物另寻买主也比较困难。

二、例信

1. Shipment

(1) Discuss terms of shipment

Dear Sirs,

　　We thank your order of January 10th, 2004, but ask for some changes in terms of shipment.

　　In regard to the port of loading, we suggest Dalian instead of Qingdao, so as to reduce domestic transportation cost. As you know, our manufacturer is in Shenyang, China, Close to Dalian port.

　　Besides, the facilities at Dalian port are advanced and loading efficiency is very high.

　　As to the latest date of shipment, we regret to inform you that February 5, 2004 is too tight, as there is a seven-day holiday in-between during the Spring Festival of China in the end of January, 2004, it is impossible for us to get the goods ready before February 5th.

　　We shall appreciate it if you will agree to shipment before February 20th, 2004.

　　If the above is acceptable to you, let us have your reply within 7 days. We will arrange to execute your order accordingly.

Yours truly,

(2) Ask the seller to contract for carriage at the buyer's risk and expense

Dear Mr. Wang,

We are pleased to receive your Sales Contract No. 666 in duplicate against our Order No. 888 for 50,000 bottles of Tsingtao Beer.

Although the price is quoted on FCA basis, we wish to request that you sign the contract of carriage with the carrier on usual terms at our risk and expense.

When you have booked the shipping space, please advise us of the name and voyage number of the vessel, B/L No., estimated time of departure (ETD), estimated time of arrival (ETA), and any other information necessary for us to procure insurance at our end.

As the bottles of the beer are vulnerable, please pack them in specially made cases capable of with standing rough handling.

Your close cooperation in the above respects is highly appreciated.

Yours truly,

(3) Urging punctual shipment

Dear Miss Wang,

With reference to Sales Contract No. 102 covering 1000 cartons of Christmas Candles, we wish to invite your attention to the fact that shipment should be effected in October.

However, up to now, we have not received any information about it. As Christmas season is drawing near and our customers are in urgent need of these candles during the Christmas holidays, you are requested to effect punctual shipment so that we can catch the busy season. In case you fail to ship the goods according to the stipulations of the Contract No. 102 and the covering L/C No. A436, we will have to lodge a claim against you for the losses sustained by us. In that case, repeat orders will be impossible.

Please inform us immediately whether you have shipped the goods or not so that we can make some arrangements in advance.

Yours truly,

(4) Shipping instruction

Dear Sirs,

Re: Your Sales Confirmation No. C215
Covering 4,000 Dozen Shirts

We have for acknowledgement your letter dated 19th August in connection with the above subject.

In reply, we have the pleasure of informing you that the confirmed, irrevocable Letter of Credit No. 7634, amounting to $3,500 has been opened this morning through the District Bank, Ltd., Manchester. Upon receipt of the same, please arrange shipment of the goods booked by us without the least delay.

We are informed by the local shipping company that S/S "Browick" is due to sail from your city to our port on or about the 10th September and, if possible, please try your best to ship by that steamer.

Should this trial order prove satisfactory to our customers, we can assure you that repeat orders in increased quantity will be placed.

Your close cooperation in this respect will be highly appreciated. In the meantime we await your shipping advice by telex.

Yours truly,

(5) Alteration of shipping instruction

Dear Sirs,

We refer to our order LP 89/56 which should be nearing completion by this time. Owing to a strike at Oakland port, which shows no sign of letting up for some time, we ask you to change shipping destination.

We should like you to consign the goods to Seattle with no alteration in shipping date. Please confirm that you can carry out these new instructions.

Sincerely,

(6) Shipping advice

Dear Sirs,

We are pleased to inform you that your order No. ... has been shipped today by MV "Everready" which is leaving for Sydney on April 5th. We enclose our invoice in triplicate with the copy of all relevant documents and we shall present the originals of them through the Bank of China as agreed.

Sincerely yours,

Dear Sirs,
  L/C No.: 01DLC077003079 INVOICE NO.: SHMH07210

  We hereby inform you that the goods under the above mentioned credit have been shipped. The details of the shipment are stated below:

COMMODITY:	HOUSEHOLD WARES (FOUR ITEMS OF LAMPS)
NUMBER OF PACKAGES:	535 CARTONS
QUANTITY:	2140PCS
AMOUNT:	US $49,550.00
B/L NO.:	COSU54710814
VESSEL'S NAME & VOYAGE:	DA HE KOU V. 210S
SHIPMENT DATE:	Dec. 01, 2007
FROM:	SHANGHAI
TO:	DUBAI
SHIPPING MARKS:	ALABRA
	SHMHSC – 07210
	DUBAI
	C/NO. 1 – 535
NAME OF ISSUING BANK:	COMMERCIAL BANK OF DUBAI P. S. C.
L/C DATE:	Oct. 19, 2007
S/C NO.:	SHMHSC – 07210

  We are also enclosing a full set of non-negotiable shipping documents for your reference. We hope that the above-mentioned goods will arrive at your port safe and sound.

Yours Sincerely,

2. Insurance

（1）The importer ask the exporter to cover insurance

Dear Mr. Wang,
Re: Our Order No. 101 for 5,000 Pairs of Men's Shoes

  We wish to refer you to our captioned Order, from which you will see that this order is placed on CFR basis.

  As we now desire to have the shipment insured at your end, we shall be pleased if you will arrange to insure the goods on our behalf against All Risks for 110% of the invoice value, i. e., US $28,000.

  We shall refund you the premium on receipt of your debit note or, if you like, you may draw on us at sight for the amount required.

  We sincerely hope that our request will meet with your approval.

Yours faithfully,

(2) A reply to the above

Dear Mr. Smith,
Re: Your Order No. 101 for 5,000 Pairs of Men's Shoes

This is to acknowledge receipt of your letter of August 22nd, 2004, requesting us to cover insurance of the captioned goods for your account.

We are pleased to inform you that we have insured the above shipment with the People's Insurance Company of China against All Risks for US $28,000. The policy is being prepared accordingly and will be forwarded to you by the end of this week together with our debit note for the premium.

For your information, we are making arrangements to ship the 5,000 pairs of Men's Shoes by S.S. "East Wind", sailing on or about the 10 of September.

Yours truly,

(3) The buyer requires increasing the rate of insurance

Dear Sirs,
4,000 Cases of Iron Nails under Sales Contract No. 214

We refer to the 4,000 cases of iron nails under Sales Contract No. 214 and are pleased to inform you that we have established with the Bank of China, New York Branch a confirmed, irrevocable L/C No. 231 in the amount of USD 6,813, valid up to May 15th.

Please see to it that the above-mentioned goods are to be shipped before May 15th and the insurance is covered for 130% of the invoice value against All Risks. As we understand that as per your customary practice, you only insure the shipment for 10% above the invoice value, and the extra premium for additional coverage shall be for our account.

Please arrange insurance according to our request and meanwhile we are expecting your shipping advice.

Yours faithfully,

(4) A reply to the above

Dear Sirs,

We have received your letter of January 23rd, asking us to insure the captioned goods for an amount of 130% of the invoice value.

Although it is our usual practice to take out insurance for the invoice value plus 10%, we are prepared to comply with your request for getting cover for 130% of the invoice value.

But the extra premium will be for your account.

Please take note of the above.

Yours faithfully,

三、重点用语

1. 运输

（1）租船订舱

Charter steamer	租船
book shipping space	订舱

① The buyer shall undertake to charter the carrying vessel.

② After contacting the parties concerned, we wish to inform you that it is not difficult for us to book the necessary shipping space in advance.

（2）装运指示

shipping instruction	装船指示
forward instruction	装运指示

① The package should be forwarded to New York for shipment per M. S. "Donglola" not later than Friday next.

② Kindly ship the goods per S. S Red Star, sailing from Yokohama on May 6.

（3）装船通知

shipping advice	装船通知

① We inform you that we have forwarded by S. S Red Star, freight paid, five cases Gum.

② We now advice you of the shipment of thirty-five bales of cotton, by S. S East Wind for Kobe.

③ We have shipped the goods per S. S Taishan as instructed by you and enclose herewith a copy each of invoice and B/L.

（4）装运期

time of shipment	装运期
immediate shipment	立即装运
prompt shipment	立即装运
shipment as soon as possible	尽快装运
shipment by first available steamer	有船即装
shipment during October	十月装运
shipments during October	十月分几批装运

Shipment is to be made within one month after receipt of the L/C.

We'll try our best to advance shipment to September.

（5）分批和转运

partial shipment	分批装运
transshipment	转船运输

① If you agree to have the goods in two equal lots, please let us know, so that we can make arrangements accordingly.

② Please make shipment in three equal monthly installments beginning from May.

③ In case no direct steamers are available, we shall have to transship the goods to ensure delivery in time.

④ There are few direct sailings and a lot of goods have to be transshipped via Rotterdam.

2. 保险

(1) 保险条款的磋商

insure/cover   *v.* 投保，保险

insurance   *n.* 保险

coverage   *n.* 保险；承保险别，保险范围；投保额

① Please insure/cover the goods With Particular Average.

② Please insure at invoice value plus 10%.

③ Please insure for 110% of invoice value.

④ We will arrange insurance on your behalf.

⑤ We want a policy with a more extensive coverage.

⑥ Regarding insurance, the coverage is for 110% of the invoice value up to the port of destination.

(2) 保险用语

Insured amount	保险金额
Insurance rate (premium rate)	保险费率
Premium	保险费
Insurance policy	保险单
Insurance certificate	保险凭证
The People's Insurance Company of China	中国人民保险公司
China Insurance Clause	中国保险条款
Institute Cargo Clause	协会货物条款
Free From Particular Average (FPA)	平安险
With Particular Average	水渍险
All Risks	一切险
General additional risk	一般附加险
Warehouse to Warehouse Clause	仓至仓条款

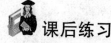 课后练习

1. Translate the following sentences into English.

(1) 货物备妥待运多时，请告知所派船名、航次及预计抵达时间，以便我方及时安排装运。

（2）我公司将于7月8日启运30箱茶具到新港，装"红星"轮于7月15日开往欧洲主要港口。

（3）现向你公司投保综合险，请将保险单寄我公司，并将费用计入我公司账户。

（4）兹通知已由"黄河"轮029航次将200箱闹钟运往你处。此货物将在新加坡转船，预定于下月初到达你方港口。

（5）现附上005号信用证项下的一套装运单据如下：

① 商业发票一式五份；

② 一份正本清洁已装船提单，空白抬头，空白背书，以申请人为被通知人，注明运费已付；

③ 普惠制产地证正本一份。

（6）由于开证延迟，无法按合同于10月装运，将延至12月。

（7）由卖方根据中国人民保险公司1981年1月1日颁布的《海洋运输货物保险条款》按发票金额110%投保一切险和战争险。

2. Write a letter as per the following particulars.

（1）8901号订单已于2005年10月17日装上"天潭"号，该船预计10月27日到达利物浦。

（2）我们已通知贵方代理 Eddis Jones。

（3）一旦贵方承兑我方汇票，我方银行代理 Westmorland Bank Ltd., High Street, Nottingham，将向你们提交提单（No. 517302）、发票（No. EH3314）和保险凭证（AR1184531）。

（4）希望这批货使贵方满意。

3. Translate the following letter into English：

我们要为下列货物按3 600美元保额投保综合险：

陶器三箱，CY 标记

该货现寄存香港第15号码头，等候装"红星"轮于7月14日起航去纽约。

我们需将该货投保到纽约，保险单准备好后希立即交给我们。请确认承保上述货物。

第九章 支 付

一、业务背景知识

1. 支付方式的比较和选择

(1) 三种常见支付方式的比较

汇款、托收、信用证结算方式是在国际贸易中使用最广、最为频繁，同时也是最为传统的结算方式。一般而言，在正常履约时，较多使用的是上述三种结算方式。

方式	分析	对卖方交单的约束或买方付款的约束	对卖方是否有利	对买方是否有利	手续	费用	资金负担
汇款	预付货款	不能约束交单	最有利	收货无保证	简单	很少	不平衡
	货到付款	不能约束付款	收款无保证	最有利	简单	很少	不平衡
托收		D/P 以交单约束付款	收款无保证	有利	稍多	稍多	不平衡
信用证		以相符单据约束银行或买方付款	有利收款有保证	交单保证是有利的	多	大	平衡

(2) 支付方式的选择原则

① 根据交易对手的信用状况选择支付方式

交易对手的资信情况对交易的顺利进行起着关键性的作用。出口商要想能够安全地收款，进口商要想安全地收货，都必须调查对方的信用。当对其信用不了解或认为其信用不佳时，尽量选择风险较小的支付方式，如信用证结算方式，或多种方式并用，如汇款方式加上保函方式等。而当对方信用好、交易风险小时，即可选择对交易双方都有利的手续少、费用少的方式。

② 根据货物的销路情况选择支付方式

对出口方来说，所销货物若是畅销货，不仅可以取得好价钱，而且可以选择对他有利的支付方式，尤其是资金占用方面对他有利的方式。而在商品滞销时，支付方式的选择权就只好让给进口商了。对进口方来说，畅销商品或盈利大的商品的交易，在支付方式选择上可做适当让步。

③ 根据贸易条件的种类选择支付方式

不同的贸易条件，对支付方式的选择也是有影响的。在实际交货（Physical Delivery）条件下，如 EXW、DAF、DDP 等，是不宜采用托收方式的，因为在这类交易中，卖方向买方直接交货，若是采用托收方式，卖方没有约束买方付款的货权，这样的托收实际上是一笔货到付款的方式。而对于推定交货（Constructive Delivery）条件，如

CIF、CFR，由于卖方可通过单据控制货权，就可以采用托收方式支付。但在 FOB 条件下，虽然买方也是凭单付款，但由于买方安排运输，货物装在买方指定的船上，也是不宜使用托收方式的。

信用证用在凭单付款的交易中，从理论上说，只能在推定交货条件下的交易中使用。因为只有这样，银行才有物权作抵押，才能控制进口商付款。

④ 根据运输单据的性质选择支付方式

货物海运时，出口商发出货物后，可以取得物权凭证——海运提单，做托收时，可以控制货物。但货物在空运、铁路运输或邮寄时，出口商得到的运输单据非物权凭证，出口商不能控制货物，是不宜使用托收的。

此外，在选择支付方式时，还应考虑销售国家或地区的商业习惯、商品竞争情况、交易数额大小、卖方在销售点是否设有代表机构等因素，以减少风险。

2. 国际贸易使用信用证结算，有关当事人间的多重权利义务关系

（1）买卖合同关系

● 买卖合同的基本当事人是买卖双方。根据《联合国国际货物销售合同公约》，他们的权利义务如下：

卖方：必须按照合同规定交付货物，移交一切与货物有关的单据并转移货物所有权。（《公约》第三十条）

买方：按照合同规定支付货物价款和收取货物。（《公约》第五十三条）

（2）跟单信用证关系

跟单信用证的基本当事人是受益人和开证行，在保兑信用证下还有保兑行。根据《跟单信用证统一惯例——2007 年修订本，国际商会第 600 号出版物》（简称 UCP600）相关规定，他们的权利义务如下：

● 受益人：接受信用证并享受其权利的一方。

● 开证行：指应申请人要求或代表自己开出信用证的银行。

开证行的责任：

① 只要规定的单据提交给指定银行或开证方，并且构成相符交单，则开证行必须承付，如果信用证为以下情形之一：

a. 信用证规定由开证行即期付款，延期付款或承兑；

b. 信用证规定由指定银行即期付款但其未付款；

c. 信用证规定由指定银行延期付款但其未承诺延期付款，或虽已承诺延期付款，但未在到期日付款；

d. 信用证规定由指定银行承兑，但其未承兑以其为付款人的汇票，或虽然承兑了汇票，但未在到期日付款。

e. 信用证规定由指定银行议付但其未议付。

② 开证行自开立信用证之时起即不可撤销地承担承付责任。

③ 指定银行承付或议付相符交单并将单据转给开证行之后，开证行即承担偿付该指定银行的责任。对承兑或延期付款信用证下相符交单金额的偿付应在到期日办理，无论

指定银行是否在到期日之前预付或购买了单据，开证行偿付指定银行的责任独立于开证行对受益人的责任。

● 保兑行：根据开证行的授权或要求对信用证加具保兑的银行。

保兑行的责任：

① 只要规定的单据提交给保兑行，或提交给其他任何指定银行或开证方，并且构成相符交单，保兑行必须：

a. 承付，如果信用证为以下情形之一：

i. 信用证规定由保兑行即期付款，延期付款或承兑；

ii. 信用证规定由另一银行即期付款但其未付款；

iii. 信用证规定由另一指定银行延期付款但其未承诺延期付款，或虽已承诺延期付款，但未在到期日付款；

iv. 信用证规定由另一指定银行承兑，但其未承兑以其为付款人的汇票，或虽然承兑了汇票，但未在到期日付款；

v. 信用证规定由另一指定银行议付但其未议付。

b. 无追索权地议付，如果信用证规定由保兑行议付。

② 保兑行自对信用证加具保兑之时起即不可撤销地承担承付或议付的责任。

③ 指定银行承付或议付相符交单并将单据转给保兑行之后，保兑行即承担偿付该指定银行的责任。对承兑或延期付款信用证下相符交单金额的偿付应在到期日办理，无论指定银行是否在到期日之前预付或购买了单据，保兑行偿付指定银行的责任独立于保兑行对受益人的责任。

④ 如果开证行授权或要求一银行对信用证加具保兑，但其并不准备照办，则其必须毫不延误地通知开证行，并可通知此信用证而不加保兑。

（3）票据关系

国际贸易结算中使用最多的票据是汇票，持票人是票据的债权人，汇票的出票人、背书人和承兑人是票据的债权人。对他们的基本权利义务的规定，各国法律基本相同。下面是《中华人民共和国票据法》的相关规定。

● 持票人：本法所称的票据权利，是指持票人向票据债务人请求支付票据金额的权力，包括付款请求权和追索权。

● 票据债务人：票据债务人在票据上签章的，按照票据所记载的事项承担票据责任。本法所称的票据责任，是指票据债务人向持票人支付票据金额的义务。

① 汇票出票人：出票人签发汇票后，即承担保证该汇票承兑和付款的责任。出票人在汇票得不到承兑或者付款时，应当向持票人清偿本法第七十条、第七十一条规定的金额和费用。

② 汇票背书人：背书人以背书转让汇票后，即承担保证其后手所持汇票承兑和付款的责任。背书人在汇票得不到承兑或者付款时，应当向持票人清偿本法第七十条、第七十一条规定的金额和费用。

③ 汇票承兑人：付款人承兑汇票后，应当承担到期付款的责任。

（4）合同与信用证和汇票

● 信用证与合同（UCP600 第四条）

① 就其性质而言，信用证与可能作为其开立基础的销售合同或其他合同是相互独立的交易，即使信用证中含有对此类合同的任何援引，银行也与该合同无关，且不受其约束。因此，银行关于承付、议付或履行信用证项下其他义务的承诺，不受申请人基于与开证行或与受益人之间的关系而产生的任何请求或抗辩的影响。

受益人在任何情况下不得利用银行之间或申请人与开证行之间的合同关系。

② 开证行应劝阻申请人试图将基础合同、形式发票等文件作为信用证组成部分的做法。

● 汇票与合同（《票据法》第十四条）

票据债务人不得以自己与出票人或者与持票人前手之间的抗辩事由，对抗持票人。但是，持票人明知存在抗辩事由而取得票据的除外。

票据债务人可以对不履行约定义务的与自己有直接债权债务关系的持票人，进行抗辩。

本法所称抗辩，是指票据债务人根据本法规定对票据债权人拒绝履行义务的行为。

3. 国际结算单据

（1）结算单据分为

货物单据，如发票、装箱单、重量单等；运输单据，如提单、航空运单、邮包收据等；保险单据；其他单据，如产地证、检验证书等。

（2）信用证业务中的单据与货物、服务或履约行为

银行处理的是单据，而不是单据可能涉及的货物、服务或履约行为。

（3）银行的审单义务

按指定行事的指定银行、保兑行（如果有的话）及开证行需审核交单，并仅基于单据本身确定其是否在表面上构成相符交单。

银行对于任何单据的形式、充分性、准确性、内容真实性、虚假性或法律效力，或对单据中规定或添加的一般或特殊条件，概不负责；银行对任何单据所代表的货物，服务或其他履约行为的描述、数量、重量、品质、状况、包装、交付、价值或其存在与否、或对发货人、承运人、货运代理人、收货人、货物的保险人或其他任何人的诚信与否、作为或不作为、清偿能力、履约或资信状况，也概不负责。

二、例信

1. Discuss Terms of Payment

（1）Asking for more favorable terms of payment

Dear Sirs,

　　We refer to your Contract No. DSG267 covering Enamelware in the amount of ＄998.00 and Contract No. BSG268 covering Basket-ware ＄895.50. As both of these contracts are each of a value of less than ＄1,000.00, we shall be glad if you agree to ship the goods to us as before on Cash Against Documents basis.

　　We hope that you will accommodate us in this respect and continue supplying us with Enamelware and Basket ware on the same basis.

　　We look forward to your early reply.

Yours truly,

（2）Reply to the above letter

Dear Sirs,

　　We are in receipt of your letter of March 8th, contents of which have been duly noted.

　　With regard to Contract Nos. DSG267 and BSG268, we agree to D/P payment terms for these contracts. However, we consider it advisable to make it clear that for future transactions D/P will only be accepted if the amount involved for each transaction is below ＄1,000.00 or its equivalent in Renminbi at the conversion rate then prevailing. If the amount exceeds that figure, payment by letter of credit will be required.

　　We wish to reiterate that it is only in view of our long friendly business relations that we extend you this accommodation. It is our sincere hope that we can enlarge the business in these lines to our mutual benefit.

Yours faithfully,

（3）Asking for more favorable terms of payment

Dear Sirs,

　　Our past purchase of Mild Steel Sheets from you has been paid as a rule by confirmed, irrevocable letter of credit. It has indeed cost us a great deal, and always ties up our funds for about four months from the moment we open the credit till the time our buyers pay us. Under the present circumstances, this question is particularly taxing owing to the tight money condition and unprecedentedly high bank interest.

　　We are sure it would greatly encourage business if you agree to easier payment terms. We propose either "Cash against Documents on arrival of goods" or "Drawing on us at three months' sight".

　　We appreciate early favorable reply.

Yours faithfully,

2. Urging establishment of a letter of credit

Dear Sirs,

<u>Our Sales Confirmation No. C215</u>

With reference to the 4,000 dozen shirts under our Sales Confirmation No. C215, we wish to draw your attention to the fact that the date of delivery is approaching, but we still have not received your covering Letter of Credit to date. Please do your utmost to expedite same, so that we may execute the order smoothly.

In order to avoid subsequent amendments, please see to it that the L/C stipulations are in exact accordance with the terms of the Contract.

We hope to receive your favorable news soon.

Yours truly,

3. Payment by L/C

(1) Buyer instructs bank

Dear Sirs,

We enclose an application form for documentary credit and shall be glad if you will arrange to open for our account with your office in London an irrevocable letter of credit for £ ... in favor of the Urban Trading Company, the credit to be valid until Nov. 30.

The credit which evidence shipment of 2,000 tons of Steels may be used against presentation of the following documents: Bill of Lading in triplicate, one copy each of Commercial Invoice, Packing List, Certificate of Insurance and Certificate of Origin. The company may draw on your London office at 60 days for each shipment.

Yours faithfully,

(2) Bank agrees to open credit

Dear Sirs,

As instructed in your fax of 2nd May we are arranging to open a letter of credit with our office in London in favor of the Urban Trading Company, valid until 30th November.

Please check our enclosed telex opening the credit to ensure that it agrees with your instructions. As soon as the credit is used we shall debit your account with the amount notified to us as having been drawn against the L/C.

We shall see to it that your instructions are carefully carried out.

Yours faithfully,

(3) Buyer notified exporter

Dear Sirs,

　　Please be informed that we have now opened an irrevocable letter of credit in your favor for £ ... with the ABC Bank, London, valid until 30th November.

　　The letter of credit authorizes you to draw at 60 days' on the bank in London for the amount of your invoice after shipment is made. Before accepting the draft, the bank will require you to produce the following documents: Bill of Lading in triplicate, Commercial Invoice, Packing List, Certificate of Insurance and Certificate of Origin. We shall expect your consignment about the middle of November.

Yours sincerely,

(4) Bank issues letter of credit

Dear Sirs,

　　On instructions from Browning & Sons, received through our Hongkong office, we have opened an irrevocable letter of credit for £ ... in your favor, valid until 30th November. You have authority to draw on us at 60 days' against this credit for the amount of your invoice upon shipment of 2,000 tons of Steels to Browning & Sons.

　　Your drafts must be accompanied by the following documents, which are to be delivered to us against our acceptance of the draft: Bill of Lading in triplicate, Commercial Invoice, Insurance Certificate and Certificate of Origin.

　　Provided you fulfill the terms of the credit we will accept and pay at maturity the draft presented to us under this credit and, if required, provide discounting facilities at current rates.

Yours faithfully,

Letter of credit

ABC Bank..., London, International Division　　　　Tel... Fax...
　　　　　　　　　　　　　　　　　　　　　　　　　Date: ...

Irrevocable Letter of Credit	Credit No. of Issuing Bank... of Advising Bank...
Advising Bank Bank of China, Xian China	Applicant Browning & Sons ... Street, London Britain
Beneficiary Urban Trading Corporation ... Street, Xian	Amount £ ... only Expiry 30 November, 2009 in China

Dear Sirs,

 We hereby issue in your favor this Irrevocable L/C available by your draft at 60 days drawn on us, for 100% of Invoice value accompanied by the following documents:

— Signed Invoice 3 copies certifying that the goods are in accordance with Contract No. ...

— Insurance certificate for invoice amount plus 10%.

— Clean shipped on board Bills of Lading in complete set issued to order and blank endorsed marked "Freight Paid".

— Packing List

Covering: 2,000 tons Steels (CIF Southampton)

Dispatch/Shipment from China port to Southampton	
Partial Shipment Permitted	Transshipment permitted
Special Conditions: We hereby engage that payment will be duly made against documents presented in conformity with the terms of this credit. Yours faithfully, Bank ..., London International Division /countersigned/	Advising Bank's notification We hereby advise this credit without any engagement on our part. Bank of f China, Xian (signed) 20 April, 2009

(5) Amending letter of credit

Dear Sirs,

 We have today received LC No. AC-3 covering the shipment of 2,000 tons of Steel. After we have checked the L/C carefully, we request you to make the following amendments:

 1. The quantity should read: 2,000 metric tons (5% more or less at Seller's option).

 2. Partial shipment and transshipment allowed.

 3. The last shipment date to be extended to end November and the validity of the credit to December 15th.

 Please confirm the amendments by fax, so that we may arrange shipment accordingly.

Yours faithfully,

(6) Exporter presents documents

Dear Sirs,

　　Referring to your advice of 10th May, we enclose shipping documents for the consignment of 2,000 tons of Steels to Browning & Sons.

　　As required by them we have included all charge in our invoice, which amounts to £ ... and enclose our draft at 60 days' for this sum. We shall be glad if, after acceptance you will discount it at the current rate and remit the net amount to our account with the Bank of England, London.

　　We thank you for your help in this matter.

Yours faithfully,

(7) Bank debits buyer

Dear Sirs,

　　As instructed by your fax of 2nd May, our London office have just accepted for your account a bill for £ ... drawn by the Urban Trading Company for the consignment of 2,000 tons of Steels to you by M.V. "Star". We have debited your account with this amount and our charges amounting to £ ... .

　　The vessel left Xingang on 3rd October and is due to arrive in London on 4th November. The shipping documents for the consignment are now with us and we shall be glad if you will arrange to collect them.

Yours faithfully,

(8) Bank refuses payment

Dear Sirs,

　　We refer to our L/C No. AC-3 covering 2,000 metric tons of Steels shipped on 3rd October. The shipping documents were presented to us yesterday.

　　Upon checking the above-mentioned documents we found the following discrepancies:

　　1. The invoice value includes 5% commission which is not mentioned in the letter of credit.

　　2. The documents are for the shipment of 1,000 tons of steels, but partial shipment is not allowed as stipulated in the L/C.

　　In view of these discrepancies we had to refuse to accept the draft. Now we hold the documents at your disposal and await your instructions.

Yours faithfully,

三、重点用语

1. 关于支付条件的讨论

① Payment will be made by letter of credit in London against shipping documents.

② Could you agree to payment by D/A?

③ For large orders, we insist on payment by L/C.

④ To open an L/C for such a large order as US＄50,000,000 is costly. We, therefore, ask you to accept D/P.

⑤ We suggest that payment for 50% of the total value be made by L/C, the remaining 50% by D/P.

2. 开立信用证

open/establish LC   开立信用证
issue L/C   （银行）开立信用证
in favour of   以……为受益人

> ① The buyer should open through a bank acceptable to the sellers an irrevocalble sight letter of credit to reach the sellers 30 days before the month of shipment, valid for negotiation in China until the 15th days after shipment.
>
> ② As to payment, we will ask our bankers to issue a confirmed, irrevocable LC in your favour for the total value.
>
> ③ Payment: by confirmed, irrevocable LC payable by draft at sight to be opened 30 days before the time of shipment.

3. 修改信用证

amend *vt.* 修改，改好

amendment *n.* 改正，修改；信用证修改书

① Please amend the amount of the LC to read: "USD2000".

② Please amend your LC to allow partial shipment and transhipment.

③ We request you to make the following amendments to your LC.

④ Upon receipt of your amendment to LC No. 567, we shall immediately make shipment of the goods.

4. 信用证展期

extend *vt.* 展期

extension *n.* 展期

① The last shipment date should be extended to end November, and the validity of the credit to December 15th.

② We regret to learn that you are unable to extend the LC.

③ We have cabled you today asking for a two-week extension of the LC.

④ We write to ask you to make an extension of the LC.

5. 汇票用语

draft/bill of exchange	汇票
documentary draft	跟单汇票
sight draft	即期汇票
time draft	远期汇票
banker's draft	银行汇票
commercial draft	商业汇票
issue	出票
acceptance	承兑
presentation	提示
endorsement	背书
dishonour	拒付

① Draw on us at 4 months after date with a bill of lading attached.

② We have drawn on you for $100,000 order Mitsuki Bank, at sight.

6. 结账

debit　*vt.* 记入(账户)借方

credit　*vt.* 记入(账户)贷方

① We have debited your account with our charges amounting to $1,000.

② Please credit our account with the proceeds after deducting your charges.

课后练习

1. Translate the following sentences into English.

(1) 正如在谈判时我们已经说过的,货款必须以保兑的、不可撤销的、凭即期汇票支付的信用证支付。

(2) 我们已按通常的付款条件,向你方开具60天期汇票,并将汇票及装运单证交给我方银行。

(3) 如果你方渴望提前交货,我们只能分批装运,即9月份装运10台,其余10台在10月份装运,望你方能同意此安排。如可行,请修改有关信用证为允许分批装运,同时通知我方。

(4) 盼传真展期你方信用证装船期至5月15日,有效期至5月30日,以便我方装运上述货物。

(5) 为促成这笔交易,我方准备接受50%用信用证,余额部分用即期付款交单方式支付。

(6) 6月12日我们曾去函要求贵公司支付拖欠的……美元,但至今未收到贵公司就这一问题的答复,希望贵公司能尽快将拖欠的账目付清。

2. Write to Bank of England asking them to open an irrevocable letter of credit for £3,000 in favor of Star Ltd. to cover a consignment of Steels. The credit is to be available for one month from the date of the letter of credit. The supplier's draft at 60 days will be accepted by the bank's correspondent in India.

3. Write a letter for Star Ltd. to the correspondent bank giving details of the shipment and enclosing shipping documents together with draft for their acceptance.

4. Translate the following letter into English.

突尼克先生:

事由:不可撤销的跟单信用证 0088 – IA 号

我方已经收到上述根据 123 号销售合同开立的信用证。经审查其中的条款,我们发现信用证条款与合同条款之间有些不符。此外,还有一些条款不符合国际贸易惯例。因此,请贵方修改信用证以便我们顺利地执行合同。

1. 汇票的受票人应是"日本大阪 ABC 银行",而不是"日本大阪 XYZ 公司"。

2. 将以数字和文字表示的总金额分别改为:USD14557.80 和 US DOLLARS FOURTEEN THOUSAND FIVE HUNDRED AND FIFTY SEVEN AND CENTS EIGHTY ONLY。

3. 将目的港由神户改为日本大阪。

4. 删除保险条款,即:出具保险单一式三份,按照中国人民保险公司1981年1月1日的海洋运输货物保险条款和发票金额的110%投保一切险。

5. 到期地点应为中国而不是日本。

6. 将"不允许分批装运"改为"允许分相等的两批装运"。

7. 全套正本清洁海运提单应注明"运费到付",取代原来的"运费已付"的规定。

由于装运期日益临近,请速修改信用证。否则,我方无法在规定的期限内发运你方所订购的保温瓶胆。

我们盼望早日收到你方的修改通知。

此致

敬礼

第六单元　争议的解决

第十章 索赔理赔

国际贸易程序复杂,涉及面广,即使非常谨慎也难免产生纠纷。一旦发生纠纷,受损一方当事人须分清责任,确认索赔对象,提出适当与合理的主张,以弥补损失。

买方未能得到贸易合同预期利益的情况主要有:未能收到或未能及时收到货物、到货短量、货物损坏或有品质缺陷。可能的责任方主要有卖方、承运人、保险人。

卖方索赔,通常是买方未能履行其合同义务,导致卖方蒙受损失,卖方向买方提出损害赔偿的要求。买方违约比较常见的是不开或延迟开立信用证、开证与合同不符且拒绝修改、不支付或延迟支付货款以及拒绝受领货物等。

其中买方未能按合同收到货物,原因较复杂。找出原因、明确责任方是索赔的关键。本章背景知识中以海洋运输为例,列明依据保险合同、运输合同和买卖合同,买方可以要求保险公司、承运人和卖方承担的责任。

本章的例信也主要是买方对卖方的索赔函,和卖方相应的理赔函。

一、业务背景知识

就进口商而言,索赔的对象和种类最常见的是:以出口商为对象的贸易索赔、以承运人为对象的运输索赔和以保险人为对象的保险索赔。

(一)保险索赔

货物在运输途中发生由承保范围内的风险引起的损失,可向保险公司索赔。以中国人民保险公司海洋运输货物保险条款为例:

1. 责任范围

海洋运输货物保险分为平安险、水渍险及一切险三种。被保险货物遭受损失时,该保险按照保险单上订明承保险别的条款规定,负赔偿责任。

(1)平安险

平安险负责赔偿:

① 被保险货物在运输途中由于恶劣气候,雷电、海啸、地震、洪水自然灾害造成整批货物的全部损失或推定全损。当被保险人要求赔付推定全损时,须将受损货物及其权利委付给保险公司。被保险货物用驳船运往或运离海轮的,每一驳船所装的货物可视作一个整批。

推定全损是指被保险货物的实际全损已经不可避免,或者恢复、修复受损货物以及运送货物到原定目的地的费用超过该目的地的货物价值。

② 由于运输工具遭受搁浅、触礁、沉没、互撞、与流冰或其他物体碰撞以及失火、

爆炸意外事故造成货物的全部或部分损失。

③ 在运输工具已经发生搁浅、触礁、沉没、焚毁意外事故的情况下，货物在此前后又在海上遭受恶劣气候、雷电、海啸等自然灾害所造成的部分损失。

④ 在装卸或转运时由于一件或数件货物落海造成的全部或部分损失。

⑤ 被保险人对遭受承保责任内危险的货物采取抢救、防止或减少货损的措施而支付的合理费用，但以不超过该批被救货物的保险金额为限。

⑥ 运输工具遭遇海难后，在避难港由于卸货所引起的损失以及在中途港、避难港由于卸货、存仓以及运送货物所产生的特别费用。

⑦ 共同海损的牺牲、分摊和救助费用。

⑧ 运输契约订有"船舶互撞责任"条款，根据该条款规定应由货方偿还船方的损失。

(2) 水渍险

除包括上列平安险的各项责任外，水渍险还负责被保险货物由于恶劣气候、雷电、海啸、地震、洪水自然灾害所造成的部分损失。

(3) 一切险

除包括上列平安险和水渍险的各项责任外，一切险还负责被保险货物在运输途中由于外来原因所致的全部或部分损失。

2. 除外责任

海洋运输货物保险对下列损失不负赔偿责任：

(1) 被保险人的故意行为或过失所造成的损失。

(2) 属于发货人责任所引起的损失。

(3) 在保险责任开始前，被保险货物已存在的品质不良或数量短差所造成的损失。

(4) 被保险货物的自然损耗、本质缺陷、特性以及市价跌落、运输延迟所引起的损失或费用。

(5) 本公司海洋运输货物战争险条款和货物运输罢工险条款规定的责任范围和除外责任。

3. 责任起讫

(1) 海洋运输货物险负"仓至仓"责任，自被保险货物运离保险单所载明的起运地仓库或储存处所开始运输时生效，包括正常运输过程中的海上、陆上、内河和驳船运输在内，直至该项货物到达保险单所载明目的地收货人的最后仓库或储存处所或被保险人用作分配、分派或非正常运输的其他储存处所为止。如未抵达上述仓库或储存处所，则以被保险货物在最后卸载港全部卸离海轮后满六十天为止。如在上述六十天内被保险货物需转运到非保险单所载明的目的地时，则以该项货物开始转运时终止。

(2) 由于被保险人无法控制的运输延迟、绕道、被迫卸货、重行装载、转载或承运人运用运输契约赋予的权限所作的任何航海上的变更或终止运输契约，致使被保险货物运到非保险单位所载明的目的地时，在被保险人及时将获知的情况通知保险人，并在必要时加缴保险费的情况下，本保险仍继续有效，保险责任按下列规定终止：

① 被保险货物如在非保险单所载明的目的地出售，保险责任至交货时为止，但不论任何情况，均以被保险货物在卸载港全部卸离海轮后满六十天为止。

② 被保险货物如在上述六十天期限内继续运往保险单所载原目的地或其他目的地时，保险责任仍按上述第①款的规定终止。

*注：一般外来风险和损失通常指：偷窃、短量、破碎、雨淋、受潮、受热、发霉、串味、沾污、渗漏、钩损和锈损等。

*注：如货损货差是由于承运人、受托人或其他有关方面的责任造成的，应以书面的方式向他们索赔；在进行保险索赔时涉及第三方责任，还需提供向责任方索偿的有关函电及其他必要单证和文件。

（二）运输索赔

承运人掌管货物期间，由于承运人的责任造成的损失，向承运人赔偿。

以《中华人民共和国海商法》规定为例：

第二节　承运人的责任

第四十六条

承运人对集装箱装运的货物的责任期间，是指从装货港接收货物时起至卸货港交付货物时止，货物处于承运人掌管之下的全部期间。承运人对非集装箱装运的货物的责任期间，是指从货物装上船时起至卸下船时止，货物处于承运人掌管之下的全部期间。在承运人的责任期间，货物发生灭失或者损坏，除本节另有规定外，承运人应当负赔偿责任。

前款规定，不影响承运人就非集装箱装运的货物，在装船前和卸船后所承担的责任，达成任何协议。

第四十七条

承运人在船舶开航前和开航当时，应当谨慎处理，使船舶处于适航状态，妥善配备船员、装备船舶和配备供应品，并使货舱、冷藏舱、冷气舱和其他载货处所适于并能安全收受、载运和保管货物。

第四十八条

承运人应当妥善地、谨慎地装载、搬移、积载、运输、保管、照料和卸载所运货物。

第四十九条

承运人应当按照约定的或者习惯的或者地理上的航线将货物运往卸货港。

船舶在海上为救助或者企图救助人命或者财产而发生的绕航或者其他合理绕航，不属于违反前款的规定的行为。

第五十条

货物未能在明确约定的时间内，在约定的卸货港交付的，为迟延交付。

除依照本章规定承运人不负赔偿责任的情形外，由于承运人的过失，致使货物因迟延交付而灭失或者损坏的，承运人应当负赔偿责任。

除依照本章规定承运人不负赔偿责任的情形外,由于承运人的过失,致使货物因迟延交付而遭受经济损失的,即使货物没有灭失或者损坏,承运人仍然应当负赔偿责任。

承运人未能在本条第一款规定的时间届满六十日内交付货物,有权对货物灭失提出赔偿请求的人可以认为货物已经灭失。

第五十一条

在责任期间货物发生的灭失或者损坏是由于下列原因之一造成的承运人不负赔偿责任:

1. 船长、船员、引航员或者承运人的其他受雇人在驾驶船舶或者管理船舶中的过失;
2. 火灾,但是由于承运人本人的过失所造成的除外;
3. 天灾、海上或者其他可航水域的危险或者意外事故;
4. 战争或者武装冲突;
5. 政府或者主管部门的行为、检疫限制或者司法扣押;
6. 罢工、停工或者劳动受到限制;
7. 在海上救助或者企图救助人命或者财产;
8. 托运人、货物所有人或者他们的代理人的行为;
9. 货物的自然特性或者固有缺陷;
10. 货物包装不良或者标志欠缺、不清;
11. 经谨慎处理仍未发现的船舶潜在缺陷;
12. 非由于承运人或者承运人的受雇人、代理人的过失造成的其他原因。承运人依照前款规定免除赔偿责任的,除第2项规定的原因外,应当负举证责任。

(三) 贸易索赔

对卖方未履行合同义务造成的损失,向卖方索赔。

根据《联合国国际货物销售合同公约》,卖方义务如下:

1. 在合同约定的时间、地点交付货物的义务

交付货物既包括实际交货,即由卖方将货物置于买方实际占有之下,也包括象征性交货,即由卖方将控制货物的单据交给买方,由买方在指定地点凭单据向承运人提货。

2. 质量担保义务

是指卖方交付的货物必须与合同约定的数量、质量、规格相符,并须按照合同所规定的方式装箱或包装。

3. 权利担保义务

卖方保证对其出售的货物享有完全的所有权,该货物必须是第三方不能提出任何权利或要求的货物,如不存在任何未向买方透露的担保物权。

卖方保证其出售的货物没有侵犯任何第三人的工业产权和知识产权。卖方仅对依据买方所在地或者订立合同时已知转售第三国法律提起的知识产权请求负担保义务。

4. 交付单据的义务

二、例信

1. Complaint concerning non-delivery

Dear Mr. ...

We regret very much that it is necessary to complain about the non-delivery of the 10,000 tons of sugar under Contract BC – 023.

In the above contract, the importance of delivery by the end of April is stressed. Failure to receive the sugar on time is causing serious inconvenience to the users. We, therefore, trust that you will look into the matter and let us know when the sugar can be expected.

Yours sincerely,

(Reply)

Dear Mr. ...

We were surprised to learn from your letter of 30th April that the 10,000 tons of Sugar have not reached you. The sugar was dispatched by rail on 28th April from Guangzhou and should have reached you the same day.

We very much regret the delayed delivery and the inconvenience it is causing you. We have already taken up the matter with the railway authorities at this end and as soon as we have any information we will fax you.

Meanwhile, may we suggest that you make similar enquiries at your end.

Yours sincerely,

2. Complaint concerning quality

Dear Mr. ...

We have recently received a number of complaints from customers about your serge. The serges clearly do not match the samples you left with us.

The serges complained about are part of the batch of 100 pieces of 50 yards supplied to our Order No. AD – 190 of May 10th. We have ourselves examined some of the serge complained about and there is little doubt that some of them are shrinkable and others not color fast.

We are therefore writing to ask you to accept return of the unsold balance of the batch referred to, amounting to 35 pieces in all, and to replace them by serge of the same quality as the sample.

Yours sincerely,

(Reply accepting complaint)

Dear Mr. ...

We are sorry to learn from your fax of 30th May that you find our serge supplied to your order of 10th May not up to the sample.

From what you say it seems possible that a mistake has been made in the dispatch of the materials meant for you and we are arranging for our representative in Paris to call on you within next week to examine the faulty materials.

If the quality of the materials delivered is found inferior to that of the sample, you can rely on us to replace the unsold part of the batch, and we shall do everything we can to ensure that such a mistake does not happen again.

Yours sincerely,

(Reply rejecting complaint)

Dear Mr. ...

We have received your fax of 30th May and very much regret that some of your customers are dissatisfied with our serge supplied to your Order No. AD-190.

We have been manufacturing for many years and can claim to produce a material that no competitor has yet succeeded in producing at the price quoted. The reputation enjoyed by our serge on international markets testifies to their high quality. From what you say it would seem that some of the materials escaped the examination we normally give to all materials in our inspection department.

We can understand your problem, but regret that we cannot accept your suggestion to take back all the unsold serge from the batch about which you complain. Indeed, there should be no need for this since it is unlikely that the number of faulty serge can be very large. We will of course replace any piece of serge found not to be satisfactory and on this particular batch we are prepared to allow you a special discount of 5% to compensate for your trouble.

Yours sincerely,

3. Complaint concerning damaged goods

Dear Mr. ...

Our Order No. U89

The 100 Coffee Sets supplied to the above order were delivered yesterday, but we regret that 15 sets were badly damaged.

The packages containing the coffee sets appeared to be in good condition and we accepted and signed for them without question. We unpacked the coffee sets with great care and can only assume that the damage must be due to careless handling at some stage prior to packing.

We shall be glad if you will replace all 15 sets as soon as you can. Meanwhile, we have put the damaged coffee sets aside in case you need them to support a claim on your suppliers for compensation.

Yours sincerely,

(Reply)

Dear Mr. ...

Your Order No. U89

We are sorry to learn from your letter of the 5th that some of the coffee sets supplied to the above order were damaged when they reached you. We will certainly replace them and have in fact instructed our Beijing Branch to send them by parcel post.

We regret the need for you to write to us and will do our best to improve our methods of handling so as to avoid further inconvenience to any customer. It will not be necessary for you to keep the damaged coffee sets and they can be destroyed.

Yours sincerely,

4. Complaint concerning wrong dispatch

Dear Sirs,

We have received your goods covering our Order No. 555 of May 5. Upon opening the cases we found case No. 99 contained completely different articles.

As we are in urgent need of the articles, we ask you to arrange for the dispatch of the replacements at once.

A list of the contents of the wrongly dispatched case is attached. Please let us know what you want us to do with them.

Yours sincerely,

(Reply)

Dear Sirs,

We are very sorry to hear that case No. 99 under your order No. 555 arrived with wrong articles. We have arranged for the right goods to be dispatched to you at once. Relative documents will be sent to you by fax.

Please keep the wrongly dispatched case No. 99 until our forwarding agent takes delivery of it, and accept our apologies for the trouble you have been put to.

Sincerely,

5. Claim for shortweight

Dear Mr. ...

Chemical Fertilizer under Contract 904567

The above Chemical Fertilizer arrived safely at Qingdao on schedule but was found short-delivered.

On checking the ship's draft by the local Commodity Inspection Corporation and after due deductions made, a short weight of 60 tons was determined and certified as against the invoice weight of ... tons after deducting 1% allowance and moisture. We, therefore, have to lodge a claim on your company for the shortweight as follows:

FOB value of the short delivered goods	US $ 897.65
Freight	2000.00
Insurance Premium	5.60
Inspection fees	300.00
Total	3203.25

We enclose Inspection Certificate No. 67/098 and a copy of the survey report on weight by draft. Please examine them and make due compensation for our loss.

Sincerely yours,

(Reply)

Dear Mr. ...

We are sorry to learn from your fax of today that the chemical fertilizer under Contract 904567 was short delivered by 60 tons. This must have caused you some difficulty in meeting orders of your clients.

We have arranged for a check-up at the warehouse at the loading port and found that there are some 30 bags left behind broken. This was due entirely to negligence on the part of the forwarding agent. For this, we apologize.

We are ready to compensate your loss and will send you the claimed amount, US＄3203.25, by T/T. I hope this overlook on our part will not undermine our good relations.

Sincerely yours,

三、信函主要内容

1. 索赔函

索赔函应做到有理、有利、有节，既要维护自身利益，又不能损害双方长期的业务关系。提出索赔必须有充分的事实依据与法律依据，明确对方的违约责任；提出的索赔要求必须合理。

（1）直奔主题，指出损失事实

● We regret to have to complain about late delivery of the captioned goods ordered on September 14th. We did not receive the goods until the end of this month though you guaranteed delivery in November.

● We have been informed by our agents in Beijing that 200 Tea Sets under the above S/C by S/S Great Wall arrived at Port Amsterdam on July 8th. Much to our regret, about 20% of the packages was seriously damaged with contents shattered to pieces and the outer bands broken.

● We have recently received a number of complaints from customers about your fountain pens. The pens are clearly not giving satisfaction, and in some cases we have had to refund the purchase price.

● We regret that the chemical fertilizer under Contract No. 123 shipped by MV "Red star" is short by 1860 lbs.

（2）充分举证，明确责任

● A thorough examination showed that the broken bags were due to improper packing, for which the suppliers should be definitely responsible.

● We enclose herewith Survey Report No. (75)366 issued by the Shanghai Commodity Inspection Bureau certifying that the quality of the above-mentioned goods is much inferior to that of the sample sent previously.

● Unfortunately when we opened this case we found it contained completely different articles, and we can only presume that a mistake was made and the contents of this case were for another order.

(3) 提出赔偿方案
- As we need the articles ordered to complete our range of cutlery, please make arrangements to dispatch the missing items at once.
- Under such circumstances, we would like you to refund the money we have paid you for these machines.
- Although the quality of these goods is not up to that of our usual standard, we are willing to accept the goods if you will reduce the price, say 5%.
- On the basis of the SCIB's Survey Report, we hereby register our claim with you as follows:

Our claim on short-delivered quantity	Stg. 357.00
Plus survey charges	Stg. 25.00
Total amount of claim	Stg. 382.00

2. 理赔函

接到进口商索赔,出口商应从以下几方面考量是否接受索赔:①是否超过索赔期限;②索赔依据是否完整,是否符合合同和法律的规定、有关证据是否由规定的机构出具;③寻找致损原因,分清损失是否由自身责任造成;④索赔金额是否合理。

在没有超过索赔期限,证据充分,损失确系由出口商造成的情况下,出口商应给予进口商合理补偿。理赔应迅速及时。

(1) 对索赔事件表示遗憾
- Your letter of July 8th complaining about the pens supplied to your order No. 45454 has caused us a good deal of concern. We are nevertheless very glad that you brought the matter to our notice.
- With reference to your letter of September 6th in which a claim has been lodged for a short delivery of 1800 lbs. chemical fertilizer, we wish to express our deepest regret over the unfortunate incident.

(2) 说明本方的调查工作及结果
- After a check-up by our staff at the warehouse in Glasgow, it was found that some 40 bags had not been packed in 5-ply strong paper bags as stipulated in the contract, resulting in breakage during transit.
- We have looked into the matter and found that we did make a mistake in putting the order together.
- We ourselves have since tested a number of pens from the production batch you refer to and agree that they are not perfect. The defects have been traced to a fault in one of the machines and this has now been put right.
- We have compared your sample piece with reference sample of the worsted cloth supplied and find the qualities are identical. This has been confirmed by the manufacturer, who assures us that both were taken from his stock of the same grade.

- We have looked up the matter in our records, and so far as we can find, the goods in question were in first-class condition when they left here, as was evidenced by the Bill of Lading. It is, therefore, quite obvious that the damage complained of must have taken place in transit.
- We have sent our representative to your end to investigate the matter in detail. We would not file any comment before our representative inspects the goods.

（3）表示赔偿（接受索赔时）

- We are arranging to send you 156 pens to replace the unsold balance 150. Please return them to us by the first available steamer, carriage forward. The extra 6 pens we are sending you without charge will enable you to provide free replacement of any further pens about which you may receive complaints.
- We will pay the amount of claim i. e. £ 382.00 by check into your account with the Bank of China upon receipt of your agreement.
- We have arranged for the right goods to be dispatched to you at once. Relative documents will be mailed as soon as they are ready.

（4）表示道歉（接受索赔时）

- Please accept our apologies for the trouble caused to you by the error.
- We wish to express our deepest regret over the unfortunate incident. You must have had much difficulty in meeting the orders of your clients.

（5）拒绝或建议其他解决方案（部分或全部拒绝买方索赔时）

- We regret to tell you that your claim can't be entertained as it is raised far beyond the time limit stipulated in the contract.
- We suggest you take up the matter with the shipping company or the insurers who have covered you on the said consignment against Risk of Breakage.
- We are prepared to make you a reasonable compensation, but not for the amount of you claimed, because we cannot see the reason why the loss should be 50% more than the actual value of the goods. Please reconsider the matter.

四、重点用语

1. 提出索赔

claim from sb. certain amount	向某人索赔一定金额
claim on sb. for …	向某人索赔
register a claim	
file a claim	
lodge a claim against/with sb.	向某人提出索赔
raise a claim	

① The goods are short-landed by 55,000 kilos, we, therefore, raise a claim against you.

② Buyer lodged a claim on this shipment for Stg. 500 on account of short weight.

③ Having suffered heavy losses, we cannot but claim from you US $ 500.

④ We claimed on the shipping company for the recovery of the loss.

2. 短重

short   *a.* 短缺的，不足的

shortage   *n.* 不足，缺少

short-delivered   *a.* 短交的

short-landed   *a.* 短卸的

① This shipment is short 1,540 lbs.

② The total shortage amounts to 1,540 lbs.

③ There is a shortage of 1,540 lbs in this shipment.

④ The goods are short-delivered by 1,540 lbs.

3. 品质缺陷

① The goods are not in accordance with the sample.

② The quality is not equal to the sample.

③ The goods are inferior to the sample.

④ The goods are not up to the standard.

 课后练习

1. Translate the following sentences into English.

（1）到货中有破包 50 个，我们以上海商品检验局的检验报告为依据，向你方提出索赔。

（2）现随函附寄上海商品检验局第 5678 号检验报告，证明上列货物的品质比以前送来的样品要差得多。

（3）由于这批货对我方完全无用，必须要求你方归还这批货的发票金额和商检费用共计……。

（4）谅你方会迅速处理这件索赔。一俟索赔解决，我方当立即将货物退回，一切费用由你方负担。

（5）在索赔了结以前，该货暂由我方代为寄存仓库并保险，所需仓储和保险费日后向你方收取。

（6）兹随函寄去 123 号支票一张，计 1 146 美元，用以最终并全部了结此索赔案。收到后请及时函告我方。

（7）我们保证该批货物发货时状况良好，有清洁提单证明。该损害可能是在运输过程中产生的，贵方应向船运公司索赔。

2. Write a letter of complaint to the supplier, informing them that many of the vases delivered on 7th September were broken and that the packing appears to have been at fault. Ask them

to replace the broken ware.

2. Translate the following letter into English.

XX 先生：

  8月1日第 AG-3 号合同项下小麦，定于10月底以前交货，你方并在合同中保证提前交货，作为合同签订的条件，但小麦至今尚未发运，对此我们深感遗憾。

  此次交货迟延已不是第一次。由于一再发生迟交，我方不得不指出：在这种情况下，我们双方的业务往来恐难长期持续。

  切望上述情况能促使贵公司设法最终解决按期交货问题。

  此致

敬礼

课后练习题部分参考答案

第二章

由于篇幅所限，这里只给出信用证修改函答案，其他业务程序、信函和单证可自行设计。

Dear Mr. Trooborg,

Thank you for your L/C No. AM/VA07721SLC issued by F. Van Lanschot Bankers N. V. dated April 18, 2008.

However, we have found the following discrepancies after checking with our S/C No. 08HY-TIV0373:

1) 31D Date and place of expiry

The expiry date should be extended to 080615 as contracted to be 15 days after shipment.

The expiry place should be China as contracted, instead of Netherlands.

2) 59 Beneficiary

Our address is Mayling Plaza, not Maying Plaza.

3) 42C Draft at

The draft should be paid at sight as contracted, instead of at 30 days after sight.

4) 44C Latest date of ship

Latest date of shipment should be 080531 as contracted, instead of 080525.

5) 45A Descript. of goods and/or services

The total quantity should be 2080 sets instead of 2088 sets as you have confirmed to adjust so.

6) 46A Documents required

+ Please amend "quality inspection certificate issued and signed by the applicant" to "quality inspection certificate issued by China Entry-Exit Inspection and Quarantine Bureau".

+ We have also noticed that you increased the insurance amount to 120% of full CIF value instead of 110%. This will incur the additional premium, which is contracted to be borne by you. Please confirm the change.

7) 71B Charges

The opening fee is to be borne by applicant according to the usual practices. So please amend to "All banking charges outside Netherlands are for beneficiary's account".

Please let us have the L/C Amendment soon so that we can effect shipment within the contracted time.

Yours sincerely,

第三章

1. Translate the following sentences into English.

(1) A few months ago we had the opportunity to see a display of your products at the Shanghai Expo and we were most impressed with their quality and low prices.

(2) Referring to your letter of December 3rd, 2008, we are glad to learn that you wish to enter into trade relations with our corporation in the line of textiles.

(3) In order to give you a general idea of our canned goods, we are sending you by separate airmail a copy of our latest catalogue. Quotations and samples will be sent to you upon receipt of your specific enquiries.

(4) Our prospective customer Messrs E. Sheen & Co. has given us your name as a banking reference. We, therefore, would appreciate it if you would furnish us with your opinion on the financial status and reliability of the above company.

(5) Though the corporation is an old establishment, losses have been incurred for the latest 3 years in succession in the enterprise, their liabilities have reached $150,000,000 and they have always delayed their payment in the past three years, it appears to us that the corporation's losses were due to their bad management.

(6) Our records show that they have never failed to meet our bills since they opened an account with us. The monthly limit of credit that we feel we may safely grant them is approximately £3,000. In addition, they are enjoying a good reputation in the business circles for their sincere attitude toward trade and punctuality in meeting obligations.

2. Translate the letter into English.

Dear Mr. ...,

We are one of the leading confectioners of this city, and have extensive connections with food stores of different cities. To make cakes and sweets, we need a regular supply of walnut meat. We have so far imported from Southeast Asia. But the supply has become unreliable recently owing to price fluctuations. We, therefore, would like to establish direct business relations with you.

Please send us an offer for 3 tons walnut meat, second grade, for delivery in September with related trade terms and conditions.

About our credit standing, please refer to our correspondent bank, Bank of London....

We look forward to establishing business relationship with you at an early date.

Yours faithfully,

3. Begin a letter to a foreign firm by identifying yourself and then stating that you want a brochure on their fine chemicals. Conclude the letter with a request.

> Dear Sirs,
>
> We are one of the principal chemicals importers in South China and are interested in your fine chemicals. We shall be glad if you will send us one copy each of your latest catalogue and current price list.
>
> Sincerely yours,

4. Write a brief but courteous letter sending the catalogue and price list requested by the receiver in previous letter.

> Dear Mr. ... ,
>
> We are very pleased to receive your letter of June 5th and, as requested, enclose a copy of our latest catalogue and price list.
>
> We look forward to hearing from you again.
>
> Yours sincerely,

第四章

1. Translate the following sentences into English.

(1) There is a steady demand here for gloves of high quality at moderate prices. Will you please send us a copy of your glove catalogue, with details of your prices and terms of payment? It could be most helpful if you supply samples of these gloves at the same time.

(2) If you can supply MP4 players of the type and quality required, we may place regular orders for large quantities with you.

(3) We should be much obliged if you could quote the best CIFC5% Shanghai price, and indicate the respective quantities and various sizes that you could supply for prompt shipment.

(4) We are pleased to enclose our latest brochure. You could also make purchases online at http://jacksonbro.com.

(5) Here in European market, only all-cotton bed sheets are salable and any synthetic fiber or blended fiber is not in demand.

(6) These prices are quoted on FOB Qingdao basis, without engagement, including packing cost.

2. Write to Atlanta Nuts Co., asking for detailed information about the kind of nuts available at the moment and the terms and conditions for prompt delivery.

> Dear Sirs,
>
> We are Nuts and Kernels importers in this country. As Christmas is approaching, high-quality Walnut Meat and Peanuts are selling well. Please offer the above nuts available at the moment, with full details of your terms and conditions for prompt delivery.
>
> We await your affirmative reply.
>
> Yours faithfully,

3. Write a letter to invite a firm offer for the following items on the seller's catalogue.

Dear Mr. ...

Thank you for the catalogue you sent us on April 3rd. We would like to have your firm offer for 2 items on your catalogue: Fancy Buttons No. 12 and No. 81 for spring coats.

Please offer them on FOB China Port basis, specifying your minimum export quantities, stating the packing, weights, deliveries and other essential details.

We look forward to your early reply.

Yours truly,

第五章

1. Translate the following sentences into English.

(1) As requested, we offer you 250 metric tons Shandong Groundnuts, Hand-picked and Ungraded at RMB 4,000 net per metric ton CFR Copenhagen or any other European Main Port for shipment during October/November, 2009.

(2) We are sending you with this letter our quotation sheet for high-quality cameras and lens.

(3) We must stress that this offer is firm for one week only because of the heavy demand for the limited supply.

(4) We are making you the following offer, subject to your reply reaching us by May 12th, Beijing time.

(5) We are very interested in the different types of MP4 Players you offer and have decided to place a trial order for the following, on the terms stated in your letter, but only if you can guarantee dispatch by the end of this month.

(6) Thank you very much for your letter of June 5th with patterns and price list. We have made our choice and take pleasure in enclosing our order No. 342.

2. Write and order for two of the items listed below, specifying quantity, unit price, total amount and terms of payment, asking for prompt shipment by parcel post.

Dear Sirs,

We thank you for the Citrocomp Software Catalogue you sent us on May 4th and are pleased to place an order with you for the following:

	Qty	Unit Price	Amount
Automatic Scorer	2	US $10.00	US $20.00

>>

(ordering No. 123 – 456)

Grammar Corrector   2 $24.00 $48.00

(ordering No. 531 – 024)

Please send them by parcel post as soon as possible and we will remit you the total amount plus postage.

Yours faithfully,

>>

3. Translate into English.

>>

Dear Mr. ...

Thank you for your enquiry of March 2nd for 2 tons of apricot kernel. We are pleased to quote as per samples sent last month as follows:

Commodity: Sweet Apricot Kernel (as per sample)
Grade: 2nd grade
Quantity: 2 metric tons
Packing: In cardboard cartons
Delivery: May/June
Payment: By L/C

As the kernel is in short supply, please send your order before the end of March. Orders reaching after the end of March will not be processed. Please understand.

Yours truly,

>>

第六章

1. Translate the following sentences into English.

(1) The cost of raw material has risen rapidly recently, so to reduce the prices by 15% as you mention in your letter will considerably lower our standards of quality.

(2) On orders for 300 pieces or more we allow a special discount of 4% and look forward to receiving your order.

(3) Our prices already make full allowance for large orders and, as I am sure you know, we operate in a highly competitive market in which we have been forced to cut our prices to the minimum. We wish we could lower our prices but unfortunately we cannot do so.

(4) We regret having to announce that beginning May 1st our export prices will be raised by 10% as a result of the recent sharp depreciation in the value of the U.S. Dollar on which our export prices are based.

(5) We are pleased to confirm having concluded with you a transaction of 30 metric tons of

groundnut kernels through the recent exchange of cables.

(6) We are enclosing the captioned contract in two originals. Please countersign and return one copy to us for our records.

2. Translate the following letter into English.

> Dear Mr. ...
>
> We confirm having received your Order No. PL – 23 for 8 tons of Vitamin C for shipment in June/July.
>
> We will dispatch the goods to you as per our agreed schedule of delivery. Shipment will be made in accordance with the conditions of our offer of April 19.
>
> We hope this order will prove satisfactory and look forward to repeating orders.
>
> Yours sincerely,

3. Order for computers from your customer cannot be met because the goods are out of stock. Write to express your regrets and explain why.

> Dear Mr. ...
>
> We thank you for your order No. DF – 456, but regret to tell you that the items are out of stock because of the recent rush to install personal computers in offices.
>
> We however, look forward to future connections with you.
>
> Yours sincerely,

第七章

> Contract
>
> Date:
> Contract No. :
>
> The Buyers: General Trading Company
>
> The Sellers: Tianjin Light Industrial Products Import and Export Corporation
>
> This contract is made by and between the Buyers and the Sellers; whereby the Buyers agree to buy and the Sellers agree to sell the under-mentioned goods subject to the terms and conditions as stipulated hereinafter:
>
> 1) Name of Commodity: "Flying Pigeon" Brand Bicycles
>
> 2) Specifications: Model MB28
>
> 3) Quantity: 1,000 Bicycles

4) Unit Price: At US $70 each CIF New York

5) Total Value: US $70,000 (Say US Dollars Seventy Thousand Only)

6) Packing: In wooden cases

7) Shipping Mark: At Seller's option

8) Insurance: To be covered by the Sellers for 110% of the invoice value against All Risks and War Risk.

9) Time of shipment: To be effected not later than March 31st, 2008, allowing partial shipments and transshipment.

10) Port of Shipment: Any Port of China

11) Port of Destination: New York

12) Terms of Payment: By irrevocable L/C at sight to reach the Sellers a month prior to the time of shipment and remain valid for negotiation in China until the 15th day after the final date of shipment.

13) Claim: Within 45 days after the arrival of the goods at the destination, should the quality, specifications or quantity be found not in conformity with the stipulations of the contract, except those claims for which the insurance company or the carrier is liable, the Buyers has the right to claim for compensation to the Sellers on the basis of survey reports issued by an independent public surveyor approved by the Sellers.

14) Force Majeure: The Sellers shall not be held responsible for the delay in shipment or non-delivery of the goods due to Force Majeure, which might occur during the process of manufacturing or in the course of loading or transit. The sellers shall advise the Buyers immediately of the occurrence mentioned above within fourteen days there after and the Sellers shall send by airmail to the Buyers for their acceptance a certificate of the accident.

15) Arbitration: All disputes in connection with the execution of this Contract shall be settled amicably through negotiation. In case no settlement can be reached, the case in question then may be submitted for arbitration to the Arbitration Commission of the China Council for the Promotion of International Trade in accordance with the Provisional Rules of Procedure promulgated by the said Arbitration Commission. The Arbitration award shall be final and binding upon both parties in question, and the Arbitration fee shall be borne by the losing party.

Signed in Tianjin on 5 February, 2008.

The Buyer   The Seller

_____   _____

(signature)   (signature)

第八章

1. Translate the following sentences into English.

(1) The goods are ready for shipment for a long time. Please inform us of the name, the voyage number and the ETA of the vessel to enable us to effect shipment in time.

(2) We shall have 30 cases of Tea Sets forwarded to Xingang on July 8th and loaded on MV Red Star scheduled to sail for European Main Ports on July 15th.

(3) We wish to cover the consignment against All Risks. Please send us the policy and charge the cost to our account.

(4) This is to notify you that we have shipped you today 200 cartons of alarm clocks by MV "Yellow River" V. 029. They are to be transshipped at Singapore and are expected to reach your port early next month.

(5) We are now enclosing one set of the shipping documents covering L/C No. 005 as follows:

Commercial invoice in quintuplicate;

One original clean on board ocean bill of lading, made out to order, blank endorsed and notify applicant and marked freight prepaid;

One original Certificate of Origin GSP Form A.

(6) Owing to the delay in opening the L/C, shipment can not be effected in October as contracted and should be postponed until December.

(7) Insurance is to be effected by the seller for 110% of the invoice value against All Risks and War Risks as per the relevant Ocean Marine Cargo Clause of the People's Insurance Company of China, dated January 1st, 1981.

2. Write a letter as per the following particulars.

Dear Sirs,

Re: Order No. 8901

The above order was shipped on 17th October 2005 on the S. S. Tiantan which is due in Liverpool on 27th October.

We have informed your agent, Eddis Jones, who will make arrangements for the consignment to be sent to you, as you requested.

Our bank's agents, Westmorland Bank Ltd., High Street, Nottingham, will hand over the documents which consist of bill of lading (No. 517302), invoice (No. EH3314) and insurance certificate (Ar1184531), once you have accepted our bill.

We are sure you will be delighted when you see the machines, and that they will find a ready market in your country. We look forward to hearing from you again in the near future.

Yours faithfully,

3. Translate the following letter into English.

> Dear Sirs,
>
> We wish to insure the following consignment against All Risks for the sum of US $3,600:
>
> 3 cartons of Crockery Goods, marked CY
>
> These goods are now lying at No. 15 Dock, Hong Kong waiting to be shipped by s.s. "Red Star", due to leave for New York on 14th July.
>
> We require immediate cover as far as New York and shall be glad if you let us have the policy as soon as it is ready. In the meantime please confirm that you hold the consignment covered.
>
> Yours faithfully,

第九章

1. Translate the following sentences into English.

(1) As we stated during our negotiations that payment should be made by a confirmed, irrevocable letter of credit payable by draft at sight.

(2) In keeping with our usual terms of payment we have drawn on you at 60 days and passed the draft and shipping documents to our banker.

(3) If you desire earlier delivery, we can only make a partial shipment of 10 machines in September and the remaining 10 in October. We hope this arrangement will be agreeable to you and, if so, please amend the covering credit to allow partial shipment, under advice to us.

(4) We trust you will extend by fax the shipment date of your L/C to May 15th and validity to May 30th, thus enabling us to effect shipment of the goods in question.

(5) In order to conclude this transaction, we are prepared to accept payment of 50% by L/C and the balance by D/P at sight.

(6) On June 12th, we wrote to you concerning your company's unpaid account amounting to US $.... We are concerned to have had no reply from you on this matter and would be grateful to receive your payment in full settlement of the outstanding sum without further delay.

2. Write to Bank of England asking them to open an irrevocable letter of credit for £ 3,000 in favor of Star Ltd. to cover a consignment of Steels. The credit is to be available for one month from the date of the letter of credit. The supplier's draft at 60 days will be accepted by the bank's correspondent in India.

Dear Sirs,

We enclose an application for credit and shall be glad if you will open for our account with your correspondent in India an irrevocable letter of credit for £ 3,000 in favor of Star Ltd., the credit to be valid for one month from the date of letter of credit.

The credit evidences shipment of 2,000 tons of steels, and may be used against presentation of the following documents:

…

Star Ltd. may draw on your correspondent in India at 60 days' for the shipment.

Yours faithfully,

3. Write a letter for Star Ltd. to the correspondent bank giving details of the shipment and enclosing shipping documents together with draft for their acceptance.

Dear Sirs,

We enclose shipping documents for the consignment of 3,000 tons of steels to ABC Company in Rangoon, dispatched from Bombay on July 3rd.

As required by the relevant L/C, we enclose our draft at 60 days' for the total amount, for your acceptance.

Yours faithfully,

4. Translate the following letter into English.

Dear Mr. Tunik,

Irrevocable Documentary Credit No. 0088 – IA

We have received the captioned L/C against our Sales Contract No. 123. After going over the L/C clauses, we have found some discrepancies between your L/C stipulations and the terms and conditions of our Sales Contract. Besides, some terms do not conform to the international trading practices. Therefore, you are requested to amend the L/C accordingly so that we can execute our contract smoothly.

The drawee of the draft should be "ABC Bank, Osaka, Japan", not "XYZ Co., Osaka, Japan".

Amend the amount both in figures and in words to read: "USD14557.80(US DOLLARS FOURTEEN THOUSAND FIVE HUNDRED AND FIFTY SEVEN AND CENTS EIGHTY ONLY.)" respectively.

Change the port of destination from "Kobe" to "Osaka, Japan".

Delete the clause "Insurance Policy in triplicate covering All Risks for 110% of the total invoice value as per China Ocean Marine Cargo Clause of PICC dated 1/1/1981."

The place of expiry should be "in China" instead of "in Japan".

Change "Partial shipments prohibited" into "Partial shipments allowed in two equal lots."

Full set of clean on board ocean bills of lading should be marked "Freight Collect" to replace the original statement, i. e. "Freight Prepaid".

Since the shipment date is approaching, please amend the L/C the soonest possible. Otherwise, we cannot ship the Thermos Flask ordered by your within the time limit.

We are looking forward to receiving your amendment advice ASAP.

Yours truly,

第十章

1. Translate the following sentences into English.

(1) There are 50 bags broken in the shipment arrived. We lodge a claim with you on the basis of SCIB's Survey Report.

(2) We enclose Survey Report No. 5678 issued by the Shanghai Commodity Inspection Bureau certifying that the quality of the above-mentioned goods is much inferior to that of the sample sent previously.

(3) As this consignment is entirely useless to us, you are requested, therefore, to return us the invoice value and the inspection charges involved, totaling. . . .

(4) We trust you will settle this claim promptly. As soon as it is settled, we shall have the consignment returned to you with all expenses for your account.

(5) The above mentioned goods will be, before the claim is settled, stored temporarily at the warehouse and insured on your behalf and the expenses of storage and premium will be borne by you consequently.

(6) We therefore enclose our check No. 123 for USD1,146 in full and final settlement of you claim. Please acknowledge receipt in due course.

(7) We can assure you that the goods in question were in perfect condition when they left here, which is supported by the clean B/L. The damage must have occurred in transportation, you, therefore, should claim on shipping company.

2. Write a letter of complaint to the supplier, informing them that many of the vases delivered on 7th September were broken and that the packing appears to have been at fault. Ask them to replace the broken ware.

Dear Mr. ...

We regret to inform you that many of the Vases delivered on 7th September were broken. On inspection, the vases were found not well padded and the cartons not strong enough. We, therefore, will appreciate it if you will replace the 20 badly damaged ones.

Sincerely,

3. Translate the following letter into English.

Dear Mr. ...

We regret very much that the wheat under Contract No. AG – 3 of August 1st scheduled to be delivered by the end of October is up to this moment not dispatched, in spite of the fact that you guaranteed an earlier delivery in the contract which was actually signed on this understanding.

This is not the first time a delay in delivery has occurred, and the repeated occurrence of the trouble compels us to point out that our business relations may not be continued for long on this condition.

We sincerely hope that the above will make you endeavor to settle finally the problem of delivery on time.

Yours truly,

参 考 文 献

[1] 祝卫，程洁，淡英，《出口贸易模拟操作教程》，上海人民出版社，2008年。
[2] 陆墨珠，《国际商务函电》，中国商务出版社，2005年。
[3] 诸葛霖，《外贸英文书信》，对外经济贸易大学出版社，2001年。
[4] 国际商会(ICC)，《国际贸易术语解释通则® 2010》，中国民主法制出版社，2011年。
[5] 李显东，《国际民商事法律适用法——案例重述》，中国政法大学出版社，2008年。
[6] Matthias Herdegen. *International Wirtschaftsrecht* 2007. 上海人民出版社，第6版，中译本。

教师反馈及教辅申请表

　　北京大学出版社以"教材优先、学术为本、创建一流"为目标,主要为广大高等院校师生服务。为更有针对性地为广大教师服务,提升教学质量,在您确认将本书作为指定教材后,请您填好以下表格并经系主任签字盖章后寄回,我们将免费向您提供相应教辅资料。

书号/书名/作者	
您的姓名	
校/院/系	
您所讲授的课程名称	
每学期学生人数	_____人　　_____年级　　学时
您准备何时用此书授课	
您的联系地址	
邮政编码	联系电话（必填）
E-mail（必填）	
您对本书的建议：	系主任签字 盖章

我们的联系方式：

北京大学出版社经济与管理图书事业部
北京市海淀区成府路 205 号，100871
联 系 人： 徐　冰
电　　话： 010-62767312 / 62757146
传　　真： 010-62556201
电子邮件： xubingjn@yahoo.com.cn　　em@pup.cn
网　　址： http://www.pup.cn